RELIGIOUS
ROULETTE

&
OTHER DANGEROUS GAMES
CHRISTIANS PLAY

Be still, my soul: thy God doth undertake
  To guide the future as he has the past.
Thy hope, thy confidence let nothing shake;
  All now mysterious shall be bright at last.
Be still, my soul: the waves and winds still know
His voice who ruled them while he dwelt below.

—KATHARINA VON SCHLEGEL

RELIGIOUS ROULETTE

&

OTHER DANGEROUS GAMES CHRISTIANS PLAY

Page 96 – the levels of Charismatic Fellowships

merle allison johnson

Nashville   ABINGDON PRESS   New York

RELIGIOUS ROULETTE &
OTHER DANGEROUS GAMES CHRISTIANS PLAY

Library of Congress Cataloging in Publication Data

JOHNSON, MERLE ALLISON.
  Religious roulette & other dangerous
games Christians play.
  1. Prayer. I. Title.
BV210.2.J63   248'.3   74-17453

ISBN 0-687-36109-5

Scripture quotations are from the
Revised Standard Version of the Bible,
copyrighted 1946, 1952, and 1971 by
the Division of Christian Education,
National Council of Churches, and are
used by permission.

MANUFACTURED BY THE PARTHENON PRESS AT
NASHVILLE, TENNESSEE, UNITED STATES OF AMERICA

For my youngest brother
DEWEY FRANKLIN
(1941-1974),
whose tragic death
after the completion of this book
makes me more committed than ever
to these ideas.

CONTENTS

PREFACE

Sometimes writing a preface is the hardest part in authoring a book. As I wrestled with this introduction I was greatly enlightened by a television presentation. Not long ago, I saw a show based on a novel by Margaret Craven—*I Heard the Owl Call My Name*. In it a terminally ill young Anglican priest is sent to a remote Canadian Indian village. There he is to learn the meaning of suffering and the acceptance of death.

He had all of the answers dogma could supply, but his bishop felt that he needed to learn from the Indians. While the young vicar did not know the extent of his illness, his Bishop did, but decided to keep it from the young priest. A key moment in the drama occurs when one of the tribal leaders says we know and understand death because we are close to it.

Filtering in and out of the background music was the hauntingly beautiful melody of "Amazing Grace." This was done in great taste. It was vastly different from the crooning, swinging renditions of the last few years. Grace here represented something to die by. It was not an indefinable quantity—some of God's miracle magic which we could tap "if we had the faith." Grace helped the young priest to prepare to affirm suffering and death—not evade these issues. The peace and acceptance in the Indian culture communicated itself to the young priest.

In the last few lines of this book I quote a hymn. The Presbyterian parish pastor who wrote it understood what he was writing about. I thought of this hymn as I became absorbed in the Craven drama. I concluded that this approach represented the best I know in the Christian faith—it is where I have lived. In my youth it was this way—living with contradictions, disease, early death, and yet affirming always, "This is my Father's world."

It is still that way in my pastoral ministry. This is where people really live. Much of what passes for ministry today is the by-product of an affluent society, a society which can afford the luxury of religious fantasy. Theatrical tinsel and mass-media trappings remove people from experiencing the essential goodness of God in the midst of their personal suffering. The church is at its lowest ebb when it seems to continually attempt the miracle of bread. Only a society of great wealth will make heroes and heroines of those who offer temporary euphoric escape.

I shall be accused of being a debunker. This could result as much from my style as from my content. If I wrote these words in theologically sophisticated terms, the man in the pew would not understand them. Therefore, I have tried to write clearly and directly. I have made an effort to support each point with day-to-day examples. Theologians and clergymen could grasp these ideas without elaboration, but I am writing for the man in the pew. If my style at times is blunt, I hope it is also clear and makes the point. Honestly, I feel, these subjects call for such directness.

I believe that this book is needed. If a serious book has been written to refute the "miracle business," then it must have been done in such guarded terms no one ever heard of it. Perhaps this book will make some points that will be discussed and studied. If it stirs up controversy I hope good will result from it. These ideas are offered in the hope that honest and sincere Christians will consider them on their merit. Whatever weakness is here is mine. Whatever truth is here is mine through God's grace.

The present day simplistic approach to religion in books, on radio, and on television is formidable. If the

medium is the message, we are seeing a serious altera-
tion of the basic ideas of Christianity. Television per-
sonalities are becoming "images." Their philosophies
are accepted as theology by many of their followers.
Their ministry takes place on a soundstage in a city
skyscraper where they speak carefully rehearsed
words. Their eyes are dazzled by high intensity stage
lights. Do they ever really see the lonely, the old, the
sick, the dying? Is their ministry a fantasy—a good
show? Do their deeds and words serve to support the
local pastor? Or do they make his work more difficult? These are the questions I have attempted to
study in this book.

So I have written as a pastor. I have written to
challenge ideas and notions about miracles, prayer,
faith, and mustard seeds. I want to approach the subject of prayer, especially, from a different perspective.
For hundreds of years theologians have had three
words to describe the essence of our beliefs about
God. They are—God is *omnipotent* (all-powerful),
omniscient (all-knowing), and *omnipresent* (in all
places). What a man believes about God will greatly
color his concepts of prayer. The standard approach
to prayer has been to tell people "how to pray." The
suggestion is that God is all-powerful and capable of
delivering us from our difficulties. But to concentrate
on the power of God to the exclusion of his omniscience and omnipresence is deadly. This approach

12

borders on paganism. God, to the pagan world, was all power, and devotees sought ways to tap His power for their own benefit.

This, then, is not necessarily a book about *when* to pray or *how*. This book is written to challenge some less-than-Christian concepts of God and prayer. Concepts, such as "only believe," "if you have faith," and others, are being packaged and sold. They are sold wholesale over the counters of the mass media. They are being retailed by traveling performers of the religious arts.

The atmosphere grows more clouded every day with these miracle cults. I would like to debate these salesmen on their own ground—the biblical warrant for their positions. Intense spiritual confusion and neurosis is resulting from this business. One of the worst results is a breakdown in our concept of God as Jesus. described him.

I have tried to offer a positive statement after every negative example. The last chapter is a summary of the ideas which have surfaced in earlier chapters.

With the coming of increased medical institutional care, more and more people will spend their last days in these institutions. I have one all-consuming burden which concerns this work: My intent certainly is not to be vindictive or un-Christian with those whose philosophies I have challenged even though I have been quite direct. One of my chief concerns is to

13

produce a readable and biblical approach to suffering and dying. This book will have served my purpose if laypersons as well as ministers are able to put it in the hands of those who need comfort and direction.

I express my appreciation to my faithful secretaries, Helen Bayles and Mary Walker who now have assisted me in several book manuscripts. Also, I am grateful to my close friend, Mark David Inmon. He served as an invaluable aide in the final revision.

These are exciting days for Christians. There is an intense interest in honest approaches to our faith. Something good can happen to us if we can learn to affirm suffering and death as a necessary part of God's plan. And, difficult as it is, we must learn to think about God as Jesus taught us.

Toying with unsound religious ideas as a roulette wheel flirts with a stopping place is certain to create spiritual trauma. There is absolutely no greater danger for the Christian than for him to place his confidence in an understanding of God which is contrary to Jesus' description.

MERLE ALLISON JOHNSON

I
PRE-CHRISTIAN CONCEPTS OF PRAYER

They bind heavy burdens, hard to bear, and lay them on men's shoulders; but they themselves will not move them with their finger.

MATTHEW 23:4

It ought to be stated frankly that there is a noticeable and distinguishable difference in praying as a Christian should and in praying in a way which can, and should, be called pagan. While all may agree to this, the difficulty lies in determining which is which.

The term "pagan" can be used rather broadly, but for my purpose it means anything that opposes the nature of God as taught by Jesus. Now this opposition is pagan, regardless of where it appears. Unfortunately, some of the source material which confuses modern Christians about prayer is found in the Old Testament. The church has long since taught the idea of progressive revelation. This simply means that the true nature of God was better understood as the years unfolded and was ultimately personified in Jesus Christ.

Here is the problem. While the church has held to this truth, it has been unwilling to accept the practical consequences. Therefore, without carefully scrutinizing and dating proof-text passages, sincere believers have done themselves great injustice. They have predicated the burden of prayer upon inadequate concepts of God just because these concepts were found in the Bible. Unfortunately, this uncritical acceptance of pre-Christian concepts has confused the subject of Christian prayer. I hope to show that there is a real difference in the way Jesus prayed and the way prayer was pictured before his day.

This is a good place to say that the use of the term "pagan prayer" by no means infers that sincere people are pagans. Unless we discipline ourselves by the measure of Jesus' mind we may be "biblical" but at the same time pagan. To be authentically Christian, prayer is made within guidelines, within bounds, and under certain assumptions.

Much of the prayer for the recovery of the sick, good fortune to the righteous (such as for rain), or at patriotic occasions is obviously unjust and unchristian. When carefully analyzed, many such prayers prove to be much more pagan than they are Christian. There is a need today for a definition of terms and for a basic set of assumptions the Christian should possess when he prays.

The word "prayer" conjures up many images in our minds. The central one is that of a person beseeching an invisible power for aid. It is important for us to see that when men use the word "prayer" in this commonplace way that they are asking their gods (or God) for some sort of personal response.

Hollywood used to show us the typical western tough guy going out on a hillside, taking off his ten-gallon hat and placing it over his heart. He would then "pray" for the "little feller who got throwed from his horse." The "little feller" was not expected to recover, according to the old doctor in the dirty shirt. The hero would start out by saying rather timidly, "Now Lord, I ain't very good at this sort of thing. I ain't ever asked you for much, and I ain't never done much good in my life. But this little feller has been good." It was the same way he talked to his girl. He could only talk with conviction to his horse.

The next scene would usually start at sunrise (meaning that the sufferer had gone through a tough night). The "little feller" would suddenly awaken, much to the amazement of the one who had fallen asleep by the side of his bed. After a tear or two the hero, who obviously caused the deity to respond, would go out and summarily execute a few dozen bad guys by himself. (Obviously, he didn't need God's help in that matter.)

Now, this seems silly because of the fact that it is silly—silly, stupid, and pagan. It hasn't been many years past when you could see such a portrayal of prayer at a Saturday matinee. In fact, when prayer is approached in modern dramas it is safe to assume that, while the melodramatics are not as pronounced, the basic reasoning is still pretty much the same.

Why would Hollywood turn this material out? First, the understanding of the senders was, more than likely, on this level. Secondly, the understanding of the receivers was on the same frequency. They (meaning Hollywood) don't produce what is not well received—not for very long, at any rate.

There are many illustrations of this kind of prayer. I witnessed this scene recently. A certain leader in prayer circles had a basketball team which was losing at half-time. He announced that he would say a prayer during the interval. This certainly opened up half-time options most of us haven't experienced. Now whether he was joking or not (by the way, the team won), it shows a remarkable latitude in his concept of prayer. Yet such praying is also accepted by great masses of nominal Christians.

A definition of prayer in a general sense would be entreaty or petition of the deity. Thus the pray-er or the "begging one" becomes the basic understanding of the word prayer. However, prayer is, in Christian thought, the communication that exists between man and God. It is a word to describe the conduit linking man and God. It is the language in which the being called God and beings called men converse. It is a term difficult to define because we are dealing with men we can see and God who cannot be seen. In this sense prayer describes an act of faith on the part of men that the unseen is responsive in some measure.

Now that we have stated the case in general terms, we must conclude that some of this entreaty called prayer is legitimate and some is not. Some entreaty of God can be called Christian. Some is none other than pagan. In other words, some of what the world of religion calls prayer may fit under the general description above, yet still not qualify as Christian prayer. It can be just so much cowboy talk on a windy prairie, or a person cutting himself with knives (as was the case with the prophets of Baal on Mt. Carmel at their duel with Elijah). In any event, there are guidelines outside of which the activity men call Christian prayer cannot exist. Prayer outside these guidelines, no matter how well intended and serious, cannot be called Christian prayer.

I would suggest that Christian prayer is not authentic unless we can be sure we are praying wisely. Good communication normally effects a response. Trapped miners take heart when they can knock on objects and get some response from the outside world. With this image in mind I would say that authentic Christian prayer is not ever one-sided. It is communication. And communication, to be truly effective, is two-way. Such is the case with communication between God and men. God hears his people, and he responds to their pleas. He may not respond as we have asked him. However, if we understand him as we should we can better read his response. Thus, Christian praying is a person's attempt to communicate with his God within established guidelines which we believe God himself has set up. Christian praying can also mean that the initiative to communicate can begin with God. God can and does speak to man, and man responds. Abraham is an example of this, even though he was pre-Christian. In any event, Christian praying is measured in this way. It must be properly done, not so much in its form, but in its assumptions. Also, it can be a response to God which may or may not be dramatic, such as quietly following God's guidance.

Someone might respond that we need to outline a history of prayer, since we are attempting to clarify its essential and authentic meaning. The answer is that this is not as easy as it might appear. It dawned on me one day that one does not find in the Bible any orderly discussion of the subject of prayer. This is a startling fact, since prayer is the underlying activity in the God-man encounter. But the Bible has no definitive pattern of its beginnings. The genesis of most everything else is there. For example, there are subjects such as sin, salvation, atonement, and many others for which the Bible, in some manner, provides a theological foundation and an attempt at systematic thought. Not so for prayer. In fact, by the time of Jesus this subject was so confused that some of his sharpest criticism was aimed at the absurdities prayer had fallen into.

I see this as a result of many things. One is man's vanity in attempting to make God over in his (man's) own image. Another comes as a result of the complete absence of the subject as a point of study in the Old Testament. When Abraham came to the land of God's promise it is merely indicated that he prayed there. We are left to assume that he prayed much in the same way as his Semitic contemporaries. When this new-found faith and this newly called people of God came to focus in Abraham and, ultimately, in his seed, no one set about writing a book on how to pray to this God.

The same is true with Moses. He is told by God to show respect by removing his shoes. In other words, he was given no theology of prayer. Men were left to grope along as best they could with their feeble understanding of the nature of prayer, its proper bounds, limits, and levels.

Thus when the authentic Man of prayer came along,

his disciples looked at their traditions on prayer. They looked at their attitudes toward entreaty with God. And then they, as pious and well-meaning men, were so moved by the difference in their approach to prayer and that of Jesus that they asked him to teach them to pray. Until Jesus came there was very little in the way of direction in the traditions of the Jewish people as to proper procedures and attitudes in prayer. However, the disciples did not ask Jesus to teach them *new words* or *new methods*. Their plea was that he teach them to pray—period. I am quite convinced that they *needed* more than methodology. They *needed* a new dimension of *understanding*. They *needed* an overhauling of their basic understanding of what prayer was all about. They were saying that they were recipients of hazy concepts and unsound notions on the subject. I believe that they were more impressed by Jesus' insight into the nature of God than by the mechanics of his praying. The ancient world had no view of God as a person who cared and loved. God was to them a being of super power. The basic aim of heathen praying was to find a way to tap this power and make it benevolent toward oneself.

In many ways the disciples demonstrated that they had not moved very far from this concept. Some of them asked Jesus to call down fire from heaven on his enemies. Here again is the concept of power. Obviously, they were wondering why Jesus would use the power source at times, as in some of the miracles, and at other times was not willing to do so. For their infancy in prayer one cannot be harsh on these first-century men. They were not so removed from many Christians today who are still hung up on the power idea. They had a long way to go from the "God has power, let's get some of it" idea to "God knows; let's have confidence he will do what is good for us!" I believe it was a realization of their confusion that spurred them to implore, "Teach us to pray." I really think that they were asking Jesus to teach them new concepts of God's nature, not new gimmicks for tapping God's power.

All too often one hears sermons, especially from the healers, that picture God as some giant computer which, if we could just feed in the correctly punched cards, would give us an answer immediately and dramatically. Then, if we did certain things, the card (prayer), upon being slipped into the divine slot, would produce the desired "answer to our prayer." This is manifestly pagan, especially so now that we have the incarnation of God in Christ. He has taught us better.

My first encounter with this brand of "Christian praying" happened when I was fifteen. I was a soda jerk. One hot summer night about nine-thirty the pharmacist and I were closing up. The back door swung open and a woman rushed in carrying a four-year-old boy. She was in panic and begged for a doctor. The child was in a state of shock. Two small but ominous holes in his swollen leg indicated what had happened. He had been bitten by a large copperhead snake while playing in the yard outside a church. They killed the snake and rushed the child inside and laid him on their altar. Then they began to quote the verses: "only believe," "if you have faith," and "the snake will not harm you" passage in <u>Mark 16</u>. After fifteen minutes of this, the mother grabbed the child and physically had to rescue him from some of the more zealous souls. She drove ten miles through rugged country to town.

When the doctor was told that nearly forty-five minutes had elapsed he hung up the phone and came tearing through the town. He was half-dressed when he arrived. The druggist and I held the child while he lanced the wound. Only the skill of that conscientious doctor saved the child that night as he lay perilously close to death. The father finally arrived. Never on this good earth have I heard a "sermon" like that doctor delivered to him. The father was an intelligent man and a man of some means.

This marked the first, but not the last, time that I had seen people who could reason in other areas of life turn off their minds where religion was concerned. The doctor asked the mother why she decided to bring the child to him. She began to weep and told

not used in RSV

of another baby that had died of pneumonia because her church had insisted that she have faith in God, and not in medicine.

I have thought of that little boy often. I see the recurring picture of the doctor who worked with him intensely. I remember thinking, "If this is Christianity, I hate it." Since that day I have learned that it isn't, and that attitude is sheer paganism. I have been an enemy of it ever since.

One could ask, "Just where does all of this present-day confusion on prayer come from?" I really don't know, except that there is an amazing diversity in the matter of what to pray for. One thing is sure, some of the mistaken concepts about prayer come from people who read the Bible indiscriminately. By this I mean that many of the concepts which undergird much of pagan praying come from references to prayer in the Old Testament and Jesus himself corrected these things. At this point the words of the disciples make more sense than ever. They asked that Jesus give them some new concepts about prayer, not new mannerisms. Their plea seems to show their disenchantment with the old attitudes. When a person in any age seeks to base his concepts of prayer or of God on the biblical material which precedes Christ he is in great jeopardy unless he reads the passages in the light Jesus shed on them. One cannot begin to understand the nature of true prayer apart from an understanding of the nature of God, and before Christ this was only seen in fleeting moments. So some of our confusion lies at the same place as that of the disciples. They were dissatisfied with the old attitudes, and if that was true of them it should be doubly true of us today. The believer in true Christian prayer cannot go to a random passage in the Old Testament and build a case for Christian praying. *It was precisely the partial and insufficient Old Testament understanding of God that the disciples sought to improve.*

The very concepts from which the disciples sought to free themselves are left for us as they were in the Old Testament. These concepts are based on what the ancients considered the nature of their God. Naturally, these ultimately colored their ideas about prayer. Further, some of the concepts of the people around the Jews were absorbed by the Jews. Despite much that the prophets tried to do to correct these ideas, the people of God were, at times, praying as paganly as their neighbors.

There is yet another factor. Part of their distortion of prayer was due to the immature stage of development in the Jews' grasp of the nature of God. They sometimes spoke quite primitively about God. Unfortunately, this primitive understanding of the nature of God directed their concept of prayer. The Bible preserves all this material for us.

Let us look at some of the old concepts which degraded prayer as a result of inadequate representations of God. First there was the notion that God was a whimsical being who changed his mind at the slightest impulse. This idea was generally shared by all the ancient peoples in the Near East. It was assumed that God was in no way omniscient. He could not see beyond the moment. He had power to change the present circumstances, but he could not see beyond those circumstances. He was a "super being," but his superiority was in his power, not in his transcendence. Since he was a whimsical being, mortals could incite him to act benevolently on their behalf, if they caught him in the right mood. These notions of the ancients' about their God are the same ones seen and heard almost daily, dressed up in Christian veneer.

Go back to the cowboy image for a moment. The basic concept is offensive to the Christian and is not even about prayer. It is a shockingly pagan statement about the nature of God. The cowboy is saying that there is a power which can operate from out of nowhere to change an earthly situation. This power he calls God is moody and might think that the cowboy is trying to ask some favor on his own behalf. In order to correct this he reminds the deity that he "ain't very good at this sort of thing," which means he doesn't press the need for power very often. And, because of his willingness to confess his own neglect of the ritual (whatever the "this sort of thing" is intended to be),

27

he hopes his grandiose display of intercession will persuade the deity to be moved to pity and restore the person in mind.

Sometimes our cowboy friend is made to say that this is the first time he has ever really asked for anything. Here we see the idea that God is like some marvelous long-lasting battery and that the cowboy has some inherent right to request his turn at sapping some of the strength. This suggests that others have been sapping the deity of more than their proportionate amount of the power source.

This example manifests the idea that God will respond according to certain sets of stimuli. However, the problem is that one has to find the right set of stimuli to induce the desired response. All the cowboy needs to do is to find the proper key. We shall talk about the stimuli later, because they are paraded before us all the time. The important thing at this point is to ask, "Where did the notion arise that God is so fickle he can be manipulated?" One answer is that the ancient Jews were influenced by the peoples around them. They could hardly resist having their presence affect their own concepts of God. Such influence is illustrated in some of the dialogues between God and man in the Old Testament. These picture God as giving in to incessant begging. In these scenes he gets tired, breaks down, and gives in much like a father or mother might for a child. The ancient world was full of the notion that God was capricious, that he could be moved by certain stimuli, that he could be manipulated, and that the real crux of the whole affair was to find the soft spot. A real case in point is the familiar dialogue between Abraham and God over the fate of Sodom and Gomorrah found in the latter part of Genesis 18. Abraham tries to find the soft spot.

To complicate things for the Hebrews, especially in the light of this outside influence, their own traditions and primitive stories about God's nature contributed to the way they prayed. For example, it should be said quite categorically that the early Hebrews were not convinced of God's unchangeableness. Many of the earlier Old Testament stories depict God as being changeable. This quality results from his inability to see beyond the moment.

There is another story which shows this in a little different manner. In the saga of Noah in Genesis 6, the writers looked upon God as all-powerful, but not all-seeing, or all-knowing. This is not to say that God was not all-knowing, but their grasp of this truth was not clear. When the ancient writers simply say that God "saw" and that he "was sorry," they were saying that he did not and could not see before the fact. That he was sorry he made man was for the same reason —he simply didn't know that it would work out this way. The amazing thing to me is how the writers figured that a second go-around with man would be any better. Was God (who was powerful enough to cover the earth with water yet not knowing enough to see that it would come to this) simply giving it a second try? They don't indicate that he knew any more about the outcome of the new race of men than he did about the old.

Now I have heard some ingenious interpretations of this passage which attempted to explain God's sorrow in the story of Noah. Entire schemes have been advanced to clarify the meaning of "sorry" or "it repented God," etc. The traditional interpretation has been to represent this sorrow as being a legitimate reaction on the part of God. While this may satisfy some, it is ridiculous because it does not truly represent what the Christian faith says about God. The ancient writer should be permitted to speak of God the way he thought God was, but we should understand that these concepts are sometimes less than helpful to us in that they are confusing. For example, an all-knowing God doesn't come to the point of saying, "I've made a big mistake, and I better start all over." The incredible aspect to the story is that when he did start all over, his first subject, Noah, after being drunk, invoked a curse upon a segment of the human race. Obviously, this wouldn't be considered much of an improvement. Noah's behavior is certainly unworthy of emulation.

There are many values to the Noah story, and I am

not belittling it. The important thing is the way in which the writer describes God. We must permit the fact to be seen for what it is, that the God of Noah, as depicted by the writers, is one who changes his mind. The writers seem quite convinced of this. To them God is sorry about bad outcomes even of his own design. Also, he can only see the situation in the approximate time frame in which men are able to see. God looked around and saw that man was corrupt. Men could look about them and see the same thing. God didn't have any greater knowledge of the outcome than men had. However, he did have power to alter the situation. In this way he is different from his creature, man. But this seems to be the only way he is different. This view of God is also unworthy of affirmation.

Now this view of God was bound to color the concept of prayer, and it is prayer in which we are eventually interested. The idea that Noah found "favor" is the same as saying that there was something in Noah that prompted a benevolent response from God. Haven't all of us heard the pitiful cries of those in trouble who felt that a benevolent God should have found favor with them because of their right living? Haven't we heard the "Why me, Lord, I've been good" routine? This infers that God in his whimsical, moody ways has suddenly changed his relationship from favor to disfavor. Men cry out, "Why have you turned on me?" They are asking why God has turned on them or at least in their minds appeared to do so. Here is a view of God which, though expressed in the twentieth century by sincere people, is as inadequate as that in Genesis 6. In fact, I fear that some praying could be unconsciously based on this passage and others like it. It is something greatly less than Christian praying. There are many such passages in the Bible which can mislead us in prayer if these are not viewed carefully.

Believers have always adhered to some idea of progressive revelation about God. While this has been accepted as fact, we have not always been willing to follow through to a logical conclusion. If there is a progressive revelation, there is a progressive understanding. Consequently, modern man's concepts of God must not stop at inadequate views, even though they are in the Bible. We are called upon to move beyond them.

In Genesis 22 we discover the much debated Isaac drama. Here specific instructions were given by God to Abraham for Isaac's sacrifice. The movingly beautiful story ends with Abraham's faith being proven by his actions. Notice that it was proven to Abraham that he could go through with it, but, the writer quite plainly states that Abraham's test also showed something to God. The picture of God here implies that he did not and could not know Abraham's faith in any other manner. The key phrase in verse 12 is "for now I know." The plain fact is that he (God) and Abraham learned of the fidelity of Abraham's faith about the same time. Here again I am not interested in an exegesis of the passage. I am interested in early concepts of the nature of God. They obviously based their understanding of prayer on their grasp of the nature of God. Now it must be said that if the view of God which someone has today is similar to those described in these stories, it can reasonably be assumed that that person's approach to prayer will be the same—that is, just as pre-Christian.

Another illustration of the pre-Christian concept of God is that of good King Hezekiah and Isaiah's persuading God to change his mind in order to let Hezekiah live for several more years. Hezekiah had some kind of terminal illness. This will be considered at a later time. For the present, it does appear that the view of God presented here is relatively unimproved over the Abraham stories, although this episode was hundreds of years removed from Abraham.

The Psalms are filled with references inferring that God, to the Jews, was forgetful. Believing this to be true, the Jews constantly prompted God. One of the psalms will be sufficient here. We read, "Remember thy word to thy servant" (119:49). The statement was made after the psalmist had recalled his pitiful plight and had informed God of his righteousness, as if God might forget. Men have from the beginning sought to

33

prompt God. One only prompts a person who either *doesn't know* the fact or who *has forgotten.* Even worse is a god who can't be trusted. At times we humans exercise a form of judicious verbal blackmail. We do this as a pressure to assure that one remembers. This is the way some people try to force their wills on God. How often do we hear, "Now Lord, you have said in your Word thus and so. . . ." The inference is that God is a liar if he doesn't come through. We must conclude that the early men of our faith looked upon God as being forgetful. The Bible doesn't hide this inadequate view. This insufficient insight into God was not checked until the time of Jesus. How very, very important it is that twentieth-century Christians not base their understanding of God's nature on such pre-Christian concepts. But this is done. And it is one of the contributing causes of some misconceived attempts at prayer today. When men quote scripture to God it could be an unconscious prompting on their part.

Another concept of the people in the Israelite world was that God needed appeasing. This too spilled over into their lives and is reflected in some parts of the Bible. The appeasing of the deity was closely related to catering to his whims. Both were done in order that he act in benevolence toward the one praying. The sacrificial system in Leviticus has this as an undertone all the way through. I realize that the need to

34

show the holiness and righteousness of God against the depravity of man was symbolized in every ritual. While this may be true and fitting for that stage of man's spiritual journey, it does contain quite a bit of the idea that God needed to be appeased. It is interesting that this same concept is found in Greek sacrifice. The old idea of God's smelling pleasing odors from Noah's altar (Gen. 8:21) is about the same as those in Leviticus rituals. The quality of the odor was made the touchstone of whether or not the sacrifice was acceptable. In Leviticus and some of the prophets the idea is promoted that the sacrifice in some way ascends as a pleasing odor for God's nostrils. This would not be so frightening otherwise, but it is stated that unless certain regularities were adhered to, the fire of God would break out and devour people. This was said to have happened to Aaron's sons.

Regardless of one's attempts to explain away these accounts, it remains that these are inadequate views of God. Christ's understanding of God was that he did not need appeasement. Now, not for a moment am I saying that this is the entire substance of the Mosaic commandments for sacrifices. I am saying that so much of the pagan and pre-Christian carry-over of appeasing God is to be found here that one cannot posit Christian prayer on this ground.

Even though we might not like to believe it, some of the same attitudes still exist. This kind of appease-

35

ment is practiced by good and conscientious people. However, their problem is that they are not careful in their biblical basis for understanding God. A favorite expression of my boyhood days was, "Say, you must not have paid the preacher." This was often heard when things would go wrong—anything from a flat tire to lack of rain. As a preacher I've only heard that statement 4,000,206 times. It would be funny if it were not so sad. Though it is said in jest it has its roots in superstition. People still believe that when things go wrong the gods are angry, are acting up and need to be quieted down. Carry this idea through and one can see that it has been to some extent Christianized. It is like telling a child that unless he is good the devil (bogey man) will get him. "Good" means to keep on good terms with the Lord so that he can protect him. In other words the suggestion is that we are to be careful of upsetting the powers that be. Some folks on the verge of sacrilege say, "I surely hope lightning doesn't strike me." This is the same as the fire's consuming Aaron's sons.

Another inherited concept which the disciples needed to outgrow was that God was a god of limited concern. There are evidences that David never thought of God as being the God of the whole world but only the God of the nation. This is a type of theism which was quite widespread in that day. These views had not progressed, even in Jesus' day, to a satisfactory level. Jesus continually combatted the idea that God's concern was for Israel only. Even though the Jews believed in a type of monotheism which stated that there was only one God, this God's concern for only one people limited his monotheistic posture as the world's only God. In other words, if he cared only for the Jews it didn't make much difference whether he existed for the rest of the world or not. Some of the Old Testament literature made an attempt at correcting this idea, notably Jonah, but in the time of our Lord this was still the way they looked on God—as one of limited concern. This in turn would drastically affect their concept of prayer, especially of prayer for non-Jews or for one's enemies. In fact, some of the psalms had invoked God to destroy those enemies. The disciples had this same idea toward their enemies. Where did they get it? They got it from a view of God represented in the Old Testament. If it was inadequate for them, it is surely inadequate for our understanding of God.

This leads to a kindred concept they had absorbed, the use of prayer as a means of expressing one's hatred for enemies. How often do we hear overtones of true animosity toward people with whom we disagree in prayer? Usually, the deity is urged to straighten "them" out. I well remember one man who was either threatened or just plain angered by my position on a subject. At the conclusion of the service he spoke to me in the harshest of words saying, "Well, God loves you so I love you," refused to shake hands and walked off. I surely was glad that God didn't love me the way he loved me. God doesn't love grudgingly or under compulsion. It didn't dawn on him that one can't harbor animosity and be Christian. By the use of his little catch phrase, he sought to extricate himself from the need to really love me. Love became an academic fact. He had read that God loved all men and felt he should also, even though he didn't feel it.

In the Jewish culture one could freely express hatred for people by praying for their destruction. The carry-over can be found in some of the debates Christians have. All too often prayer is used to involve God in some measure in the animosity. Once a group of people sought to meet and plot to have their pastor fired at the next congregational meeting. They called their meeting a "prayer meeting" and even prayed for their victim. (During the Spanish Inquisition the same thing was done right before they lopped their enemies' heads off.) When the group in question gathered the following business meeting night, they piously opened with prayer. The pastor told me the next morning that the saddest thing was that they could pray their own wills into words which eventually, to them, represented God's stance. Their prayers were worded to bring God into the whole sordid affair. A radio preacher, obviously under quite a bit of strain with his local congregation, urged God on his Saturday program to help bring revival to his church. In his words, and I shall never forget them, "Lord, bring my board around or, Lord, just pop it to them!" This is downright hilarious but can be attributed in large measure to an unconscious absorption on his part of these pre-Christian ideas. Christians have been known to reveal really bitter animosity when in the midst of prohibition campaigns. "Drys" have been known to hate "wets"—all in the name of God.

Another lingering thought which keeps surfacing is that the disciples must have been amazed at Jesus' private prayer life. It does seem that by the time of the first century the basic concept of God was that access to him was very difficult. Access to God was greatly involved with a system of priests. God became so "holy" to the Jews at one stage that they couldn't even call his name. Surely the disciples saw a remarkable dimension in personal prayer that seemingly had disappeared in favor of prayers at stated rituals. In fact, praying had become a fine art. We have the suspicion that it was not practiced to any large degree by the masses. Here is another concept of prayer which was badly in need of correction. *They could pray!*

Another idea which they had concerning God, one which obviously carried over into their praying, was that God's presence was here today, there tomorrow, and sometimes gone completely. Isaiah says, "Seek

39

the Lord while he may be found, call upon him while he is near" (55:6). Certainly the mystery of God's accessibility and his presence must have confounded poor unlearned fishermen. In fact, I hear this passage quoted today as a fear tactic and I'm not certain what Isaiah meant. Certainly, if we called on God only when we felt that he was near this wouldn't be much comfort, and certainly it wouldn't be reliable. The assurance of his constant presence must rest on more firm ground, and it does—according to Jesus.

Another concept inherited by the disciples which still rears its ugly head today: the possibility that for some reason God will decide not to hear our pleas. Certainly there is truth to this, but it is based on our unwillingness to meet God's terms and not on his moods. In Psalm 66:19 the writer says, "But truly God has listened; he has given heed to the voice of my prayer." The important aspect to notice here is not that God listened to the psalmist but the possibility that he wouldn't listen on other occasions. The idea that one might receive a deaf ear from God was very much a factor in the notions on prayer before Jesus' day.

In Psalm 6, the writer pleads with God to turn and extricate him. He says that he has prayed every night to the extent that he has flooded his bed with his tears. Finally, he proclaims that God *has heard*.

We would say that "one walks the floor and wrings

40

his hands in distress." It is the same notion that a good bit of languishing goes into a setting before one gets through to God. Now and then we hear of "praying through." The notion represented here is that for some reason first attempts at prayer can't get the message across, and it takes a lot of urging upon God. This is popularly described by some miserable souls in the words, "I pray but I feel as if my prayers don't get through or they don't get any higher than the ceiling." Now and then we hear of prayer groups praying all night until a brother breaks through to God. This is an unconscious surfacing on their part of the hidden notion that at times God turns a deaf ear to us. However, it could be a part of their theology. Let us hope not. Most people I counsel don't know it, but they are really wanting someone to tell them that God has heard their cries. They want the assurance that this is true regardless of the way they *feel* about it. They come to declare to me their growing skepticism of prayer, but what they are really saying is that they are skeptical of the nature of God as he relates to them. They need reassurance *not about the validity of prayer but about God!* Even though their prayers are not granted the way they wish, they find some measure of peace in knowing that God hears them.

Another pre-Christian idea is a rather irrational notion about one person's ability to keep God from blessing his people. This is Christianized in the old revival preaching popularly called "sin in the camp." It goes back to an old story in Joshua 7 where a man named Achan became a thief and a curse fell on the entire settlement of God's people. After some "priestly" discernment Achan was trotted out, accused, and subsequently stoned along with his family. Then the ban was lifted.

In Numbers 16:22 the cry is lifted to God with a horrible note of uncertainty, "Shall one man sin, and wilt thou be angry with all the congregation?" In my boyhood I used to hear some spellbinding sermons based on this spooky theology. The old preachers would preach in the revivals for three or four nights and if things weren't moving as they thought they ought to, they would preach this idea. The channels to God's blessings were stopped up and someone there "was an Achan." The preacher would normally terrorize (though under God he would swear he was not) us trembling folks by threatening us with God's wrath. This usually didn't mean stoning, but we came to expect longer sermons and longer invitations. The topic would be announced as "sin in the camp," and we all knew that this would be the best night yet. He was really going to "plow some corn." That was an old euphemism for scaring hell out of the folks and scaring heaven into them. How well I remember one such occasion when the piano player, who had enough money, culture, and accessibility to "way-

True

I can Remember a sermon like this

ward ways," still had enough religion to get scared. Right in the middle of "Almost Persuaded, Doom Comes at Last," she left a dangling chord and made her way to the proper atoning position. The preacher then announced that the woman had confessed something, as I remember it, like imbibing a little bubbly at some occasion. She had now renounced the error of her ways. This was followed by a literal floodgate of similar confessions, a few Prince Albert packages left on the altar table, and the announcement that the ban was lifted. The Achan had been found. Even as a lad I doubted the reasoning of the Lord in all of this. It appeared to me that he ought not to pick on us who at least were there. The "channels" logically ought to be plugged up by those people who got to go to the movies and not by the poor sinners who at least felt the need to go to church or were made to go.

It came as a relief and a liberating feeling in later years to learn it wasn't the Lord that had his regulations all twisted; it was the preachers. This downright absurd idea was in vogue during Old Testament days, and it is disconcerting to see it parlayed into the God-man relationship today. So much for "sin in the camp"—may those tents fold up. The unnecessary guilt the church has fostered makes it a wonder that folks still come at all. Christianity is bound to be authentic having lasted through such experience.

One more pre-Christian notion was that God didn't

hear the prayers of the heathen. This meant that only the Jews could really touch God. The idea has been Christianized into sermons along the topical line, "Does God hear a sinner's prayer?" Specific statements are made that only Christians can pray. Such statements claim that the only prayer a heathen can pray is: "God make me a Christian." This is a carry-over of the one-God-for-the-one people idea, and the bold inference is that we just can't share his power with the undeserving ones. This idea is further crystalized in some denominations' belief that they are the only people of God. Heathens, to them, might even be other Christians.

These are ample reasons for the disciples to be confused to the point that they literally pleaded with Jesus to help them in this matter of prayer. Although there is a measure of truth in these pre-Christian ideas I have cited, there was not enough to do much more than muddy the water. Most of these ideas about God were antiquated by Jesus' day. Some of them were given newer dimensions by Jesus and some were refuted altogether. Many more basic pre-Christian misconceptions could be noted, but with this as a basis I would like to move closer to subjects which are coming increasingly to the front today.

It is my contention that much of the pagan praying which is done today finds its basis and stimulus from these very antiquated concepts. Men continue to be led astray much as they were before our Lord walked among them. The center of gravity for the Christian faith has always been Jesus. The need was so great to reveal the Father—truly reveal him so that men might believe—that God became flesh and dwelt among us. While God was uniquely among men in Jesus Christ some confused and bewildered men, seeing his understanding of prayer, pleaded with him that he teach them to pray! Somehow even the best of God's servants didn't know too much about prayer until the Galilean freed them from their heavy burdens. The church would do well not to bind men again.

II
THE CONTINUAL INFLUENCE
OF PAGAN PRAYING

Unless prayer is grounded upon a sound structure of belief, it becomes magic, or wishful thinking, or at best a form of therapeutic meditation.

—GEORGIA HARKNESS

I have attempted to show how it is altogether possible to trace some of our present day misconceptions about God (and thus about prayer) to pre-Christian concepts found in the Old Testament. These were embraced in the ancient world and assimilated by the Jews. Instead of the church's relegating these to their proper place, it is clear that these concepts have been accepted at face value and incorporated into what is called Christian praying. In this chapter I want to show how these pre-Christian concepts have continually influenced us in the matter of prayer and have distorted our concept of the nature of God.

Probably at no other point did Jesus raise more

objection to the traditions of his religious world than at the point of the contemporary conceptions of God. He was concerned with the effect of these concepts on the piety and the praying of the Jews. The same effects can be seen today. After Christ has made things absolutely clear about prayer we ought to be willing to call these effects what they are. There is no other way to describe prayer today when it is sub-Christian in its assumptions than to *call it pagan.* Frankly, much of the praying that is done in the name of Christ is simply pagan! In fact, some men have become proficient at this business and have even established "ministries of prayer" on these assumptions. The business has made some of them very, very rich.

When Jesus confronted a world which should to some extent have known better, he observed their attitudes at prayer and called some of them pagan. In Matthew's gospel, chapter 6, he says, "Beware of practicing your piety before men in order to be seen by them; for then you will have no reward from your Father who is in heaven . . . . And when you pray, you must not be like the hypocrites; for they love to stand and pray in the synagogues and at the street corners, that they may be seen by men . . . . And in praying do not heap up empty phrases as the Gentiles do; for they think that they will be heard for their many words. Do not be like them. . . ." (Matt. 6:1, 5, 7). He goes on to demonstrate how to pray in the Lord's Prayer section.

47

When we correctly substitute the word pagan for the word Gentile we have his thrust. Here he says, "Do not be like them"! The sad thing about it is that *we are* like them. Something which jumps out at me in this passage is that in Jesus' mind piety (the life of devotion to God) and public prayer were not synonymous. Thus, Jesus' first condemnation of pagan praying concerned the way prayer was used. For example, he maintained that prayer in public was not to be used to demonstrate one's piety. In other words, men in his day would make a demonstration of themselves at prayer in an effort to prove their devotion to God. In order to get off and running, it can be said quite categorically that even today some men pray with a wrong motive in public places. This is not done out of an inner compulsion toward the need for communion with God, but because at those moments, prayer can demonstrate their religious postures (piety).

My mind races to the many events in which men make room for an invocation or grace at meals. What prompted them to do so was how the entire affair would look if they did not pray. Upon planning a civic function a notable of one city called me and asked if I would pray. He prefaced his invitation by saying, "We almost forgot to leave a spot for some minister to come and pray, and that would have been terrible. We don't want to be looked upon as being

48

pagans." This triggered a response in my mind that prayer thrown in for this reason was probably more pagan than its omission. It was for effect and nothing more. It was the proper thing to do to further the appearance that the affair was run by men of some degree of piety. Much can be said about the inappropriateness, from a distinctly Christian point of view, of prayer at public occasions. In the main, it becomes a rather pagan exercise by virtue of the reason for its being placed on the agenda. Few are really interested in prayer as a genuine means of expression. In fact, after an hour of cocktail talk, some have begun to eat and been heard to say with a mouthful of food, "Say, have we had the blessing; I can't remember?"

Or, there is the typical banquet to announce the dedication of a new industry in town by the Chamber of Commerce. When the crowd is quieted down some soul remarks, "Let's get this show on the road." The master of ceremonies taps on his water glass and begins the ritual by a concession to the deity, to show that they have not forgotten him in the city's progress. A free meal is given to the lucky minister if he will stand and do his thing by saying a few words to God. This use of prayer as a symbol of corporate piety is in no way related to the nature of true Christian praying. Probably a moment of silent prayer would be better, if prayer is appropriate at all on such occasions. My subject here is not the place of prayer at functions like

49

this but public prayer as a demonstration of piety which Jesus strictly forbad.

Recently I read of a most refreshing invocation at such an event. It was printed in the sports section in the *Arkansas Gazette* by the sports editor, Orville Henry. It was delivered by the principal of Catholic High of Little Rock:

. . . The highlight of the opening ceremony was provided by Reverend George Tribou, whose function was to ask the blessing. Here is what he said:

"I'm sure that I was asked to call forth your blessing on these matches because I'm the only one here not particularly interested in tennis and therefore can be most objective in what to ask you for. And I ask you for four things:

"Grant that these athletes may perform with the fullness of the gifts of strength and coordination that you have given them. Teach them to be grateful for these gifts, one small portion of which would bring overwhelming joy to the weak, the crippled, and the paralyzed. Let this recognition of your generosity to them be so sharp that in their gratitude they may always be humble men. Teach them that athletic stardom is a brief thing and that the way the world measures them as tennis champions is not as important as the way they measure themselves as men.

"Grant to the referee, the linesmen, and the umpires sharpness of vision and fairness of judgment that they may see from the sides with the same clarity with which You will be watching from above.

"Grant to the spectators the insight to see the beauty and grace of athletic prowess as a reflection of the beauty and

50

grace of Your gifts to all men and women according to their needs in the divine plan.

"Finally, grant to all of us the same enthusiasm for Your communion cup that is had for the Davis Cup.

"These gifts we ask in the name of Jesus Christ, Your Son."

The sum of the remarks of Governor Bumpers, who followed Father Tribou to the microphone, was "Amen."

And Dennis Ralston, the captain of the American team, hurried over to grasp the priest's hand and murmur, "Thank you for the prayer."

So much for proper praying—back to prayer as piety.

One day years ago an incident opened to me a whole new dimension of the study of prayer as a public demonstration of piety. We often use prayer this way in violation of our Lord's commands.

Two minister friends and I went into a very busy restaurant at high noon. One of the men was pastor of a prominent church, and the other man and I were well known by some of the persons in the crowded room. It was one of those small town restaurants where the tables are very close. Also, the waitresses carry food over the heads of folks in a circus-like performance as they make their way to each table.

We spoke to several people and the customary good-natured remarks were bantered about such as that most original one: "What are you three preachers up to? Better watch it when three get together!" After

Very good [handwritten marginalia]

51

we were seated and had ordered the luncheon fare of the day, our food was eventually brought. Unknown to the "senior minister-in-charge" the bread had not been brought. Nervously, he did a thing that has taken place thousands of times. He, as our host, fumbled with his napkin and said these words, "Men, don't you think that we ought to pray; all these folks know that we are ministers, and it would set a good example." He then dropped his head and called on the other brother to say a word or two to the Lord. Now I'm sure the Lord heard him, but I could barely make it out. Though I was seated across the table, the noise of the place drowned him out. He did not notice that just as he dropped his head the poor waitress was over him with cornbread (you can't eat greens without cornbread). Not wanting to interrupt this scene of genuine piety, she froze in a statuesque display of frustration. Feeling pity for the girl, I responded by saying, "Give me the bread, I think they are busy." I reached over their bowed heads, relieved the embarrassed girl and began to eat. Now I am not sure whether I was the hero or the villain in the situation because I must confess it marked the first time I had ever had the courage not to conform to this type thing. My friends and I later laughed about the situation, and we all learned some things. Each reader will be painfully aware of episodes much like this one in his own experience.

Here is prayer being used to make an impression of sterling piety, or what could be worse, here is prayer being used to further the image of the ministerial office. I have heard public prayer used as an argument for courage. It goes like this. "We ought not to be ashamed of our God or of the fact that we are Christians, and it takes courage to pray in a public restaurant; so let's take courage and pray." It takes no courage to do this thing—it is not a matter of courage but of motive. I have heard it said that prayer in public sets the right example and syrupy illustrations are given. Stories are told of waitresses working in a place for years before they see a person pray before his meal. This is well and good, but the inference is that these are the first Christians who have been served. The impression is based on an act of prayer used as piety. Jesus said that we are not to practice our piety before men in order to be seen by them. That is exactly what this type of public prayer accomplishes, even though it be deemed to have an "evangelistic" purpose.

I feel sorry for lay persons at this point. Like a lot of men, I have contacts with lay persons from many churches through speaking engagements. It is my privilege to be taken out to restaurants as the guest of these fine people. It almost invariably is the case that an uneasy nervousness permeates the atmosphere immediately before we sit down or before we begin to eat. The lay person, not knowing exactly what to do

53

and what is appropriate, usually feels forced to call on someone to pray. All eyes in the restaurant are on "old Joe" and his guests. Others in the restaurant surmise that Joe is the host to the established clergy because we practiced a wee bit of piety in public.

I have advised my people from the pulpit to feel at ease and not to call on me to pray in a busy restaurant. I know of many other ministers who have done the same thing. There are good reasons for this. One is that all too often such prayer is in strict violation of Christian principles for praying, if it is done for effect—the affecting of a posture of piety. Also, the atmosphere is not conducive to praying as waitresses scurry around and people come and go. Jesus plainly says that personal prayers should be conducted in private. It is absolutely the fault of the ministry for a lack of clarity in such matters. Good advice to lay persons (and I especially want these words to have pastoral guidance) would be to observe the following rule. When the surroundings are not conducive to prayer, and when they cannot be altered by calming things down, it is best not to pray. But, if one insists on prayer, a one sentence statement of praise or brief, individual, silent prayer is more than adequate. Frankly, I suggest that it be left off altogether. If we are grateful, God knows our gratitude. Using prayer to show our gratitude to other men or to fulfill an expected ritual is as pagan as can be.

The use of prayer to demonstrate piety or the posture (image) of the praying one is seen in another familiar practice. It involves the matter of prayer in hospital rooms or in private residences. We are not broaching the subject of faith healing; that discussion comes later. At this point we are thinking about the expectation that prayer is to be offered by the minister at the conclusion of a visit to a hospital room or to a home. I am often amused at my doctor friends. They have a game I call the "stethoscope game." It is their badge of service when they make their visits to the rooms. Many times after looking at the charts they know that nothing of import can take place by the use of a "body feel." The patient, however, has come to expect that the doctor shouldn't just walk in and merely stand at the foot of the bed. So to further his image, the doctor takes out his stethoscope, plugs it in, looks up at the ceiling in that ponderous sort of way, feels around a bit and declares all is well.

Many times this is not important or even necessary except for the psychological benefit of the patient. He just feels cheated at having a visit if he doesn't get felt of and listened to. Sometimes, this same game carries over to the visiting minister. Before he leaves he is expected to close his visit with a "little prayer," which is like a "little feel" from the doctor. Now before the ire of some is raised to the point of needing the doctor, I must say that although prayer may be good psychology (as in the stethoscope game), this is not a valid reason for praying. It may be good psychology but it is poor theology, and what is worse, poor counseling. *It may bring false hope.* I want to cover this subject in a later discussion. At this point the emphasis is upon the use of prayer as an expected ritual, a practice of piety, or a salve for the minister's mind assuring him he has done "his work" for his people.

Pastoral letters to new church members often contain a frank statement that the ministers pray in a hospital room or elsewhere *only* if asked to pray. It has been a matter of no little concern and embarrassment that closing hospital visits with routine prayer is chaotic. When the minister uses this means of communicating to God how concerned he is for this person, it is a pagan use of prayer. God knows his concern, and if the minister needs to impress this on the patient he should frankly tell him so without the aid of an address to God for the purpose. Some of the most meaningful moments of prayer are in hospital rooms when the minister is *asked* to pray. I want to be clearly understood at this point. It can be helpful to pray in a hospital room. But simply to close a visit with prayer for the sake of effect is pagan!

A ritual we used to see in a pastoral call was the minister's closing suggestion that "we all join hands and pray." Once I asked a minister why he did this.

This was his reply: "My people expect this of me, you know, to ask a little blessing on them before I leave." My response was that this smacked of the witch doctor routine. What if God didn't wish to "bless" them? His answer was that that was God's business; his duty was to offer prayer. He said his role called for it. Here again is a use of prayer to effect and further a pietistic image. It is by its very nature a violation of Christian praying, yet it is done all of the time.

There are times to pray in homes, but it should be at the instance of a need expressed by the host. Here, as in hospital rooms or restaurants, prayer should never be a means to create an image. Most of the time it is better left undone, for when prayer is used as ostentatious piety or to play a role, it is unchristian.

We should move on to other aspects of praying which represent pagan notions. The heathen looked upon God as detached. The primary problem the heathen world faced in prayer was getting their god's attention. Once again I refer to Elijah on Carmel when he taunted the priests of Baal because Baal wouldn't answer. Elijah suggested that perhaps he was asleep and couldn't hear them. Then he said that their god was on a journey and that was why there was no response. He further suggested that he was in the bathroom (outhouse in that day—that suggestion is seen in some better translations). Elijah knew what was troubling the false priests. The pagan world did not doubt the power of their gods, only their willingness. Elijah himself later fell prey to believing that God was detached from his needs. He was not completely free from the problem he taunted the priest about.

Here is the age-old idea that Job represented and one which continues to linger with us today. Job maintained that surely God was oblivious to the existing situation. Job did not see purpose in his predicament at all. He only saw the situation as the result of God's indifference. So he seeks to focus God's eyes. His wife in desperation with God urges Job to tell God off. Her inference is that a god who couldn't remember how good a man had been and who permitted such things to happen ought to be cursed. He should be written off as unworthy of veneration.

As I mentioned previously, some people in misfortune are perplexed, not about what they have done to bring it about, but about why God has not noticed their fidelity which should have warded off misfortune. Here the implication is that someone needs to call God's attention to some factors. The idea is expanded and popularized in the slogan "Someone up there likes me." The saying implies that the steady attention of God is on such and such a person. If good has not come to said person then someone up there must not like him.

In keeping with this notion is the idea that God

needed to have his head turned in one's direction. The approach to God is like a child who says, "Daddy look at me," meaning that he has observed a brother or a sister long enough. What is worse, *God needs to be informed;* he doesn't know what is going on.

There is a place in prayers of ritual to rehearse God's mighty acts. This can take place in a prayer of praise and thanksgiving. This is something altogether different from registering a lengthy series of reminders to God as if his memory needs to be jogged. It would be better to leave much prayer verbiage unsaid rather than go into a lengthy "Lord, you know so and so" routine or a spiel frantically enumerating the needs of the hour. The Christian never prays from the standpoint that now he is going to inform the Lord of the situation at hand. Pagan praying always assumed that God needed to be brought up to date on the situation. That attitude is predicated on the idea of God's inability to see beyond the moment, as we saw in chapter 1.

Pre-Christian prayer assumed that God's generosity came as a result of certain rituals. Gods sat placidly in their precincts and watched men go through their paces. When a certain degree of satisfaction was reached the gods would act. A similar approach is seen in talk about prayer for revival. The cry "We need revival in our time," seldom incorporates a definition of revival. A preacher recently expressed the need for revival of the sanctity of the home and the end to divorce. He suggested that we need a revival of the day when the community so frowned on divorce that people were penalized by community estrangement if they were divorced. This is just one example of the way the word "revival" is used.

Usually, when campaign strategy is proposed for the purpose of bringing about a revival we hear the phrase, "If we will only pay the price, God will send us revival." We read it in literature that ought to represent better theology. The assertion is based on a concept in II Chronicles 7:14 which is used as the proof text for a formula of so-called revival. Originally the passage meant that God would bring agricultural blessings. Here are pronounced overtones of the pagan gods who watched men go through their paces. The idea that "if we will pay the price God will send down his blessings" raises serious questions for Christians, even though it may sound good from the pulpit. Does God not know that we need a revival before we become aware of it ourselves? If it is needed, why do we have to approach him as if he begrudges our getting it? The answers are obvious upon serious reflection. When we talk of God's withholding his blessings until certain things are done it smacks more of a game than a spiritual relationship. God is not interested in the multitude of burnt offerings or any "price," but contrite hearts.

60

An experience during one of my church ministries illustrates the confusion over revival. We had had a typical week of preaching, but by the fourth night we had not registered any noticeable results. A layman asked for the floor, and I gave him a few minutes at the conclusion of the service. He said that he had witnessed "success" in several past revivals where he had lived. He now wanted to give us the formula for success "if we would but pay the price." I knew what was coming. He quoted Jesus as saying that when two or three were gathered in his name he would grant their desires. I don't think this is a suitable interpretation of the passage, although I hear it used this way quite often. My friend suggested that we needed an all-night prayer meeting. This was the price we had to pay. If only one other person would join him that would make two which was the exact number Jesus had specified. He said the two of them would plead with God all night long. He further assured us that God was honor-bound to answer from heaven and unstop the drain through which he could shower his blessings. This sounded much like a spiritual drain cleaner. No one took up his suggestion, not even I, because I myself had once fallen prey to such stuff. But this example is not farfetched! This approach to God takes place all about us and represents a picture of God which is horribly pagan. Also, it infers that God can't be present with a person who is alone. The lone survivor of a plane wreck can't find much encouragement in this literal interpretation of the passage.

A frantic call to prayer says that we care more than God cares. It says that God is limited, because even though he would like to send his blessings, he can't, unless we go through some ritual such as an all-night prayer meeting. God is pictured looking down on us poor mortals saying, "I would like to bless you but you, or some of you (at least two), are going to have to pay the price of the loss of a night's sleep before I will bless."

This approach implies that the God-man relationship is tied more to ritual than to the heart. Apparently God can't "see" our concern until we prove it. On one hand, God can't bless his people without some gimmick such as "by twos" or all-night sessions. On the other hand, he doesn't really know our hearts. In order to prove something to him we are to pay the price. Having once seen what he could not previously see, he will open his storehouse of spiritual power. If this latter is true God is not "all-knowing" as he is not "all-powerful" in the former. In either case he is not God, and we are in a stage far below the level of Jesus' mind.

All-night chain prayer meetings may sound good, but they look rather pagan to me. It looks as if we don't really want God to get any sleep. Upon being relieved by our brothers, we can go to bed while they take up where we have left off begging God to send revival. Now all this seems to indicate a state of frenzy and too much concern with time. Every now and then, in a ministers' meeting someone is heard to say that the secret to a good revival is a prayer meeting all night before the Sunday the meeting starts. This prompts me to ask: "If God responds to a computerized formula for tapping Heaven's flow, then why stop?" Why not perform this rite every Saturday before every Lord's Day? We could then enjoy a good thing each week. In fact, if the riddle is solvable by this method, it is almost a sin not to keep the prayer chain each Saturday night!

In my first church the formula-approach was in vogue. That was in 1952. It reared its head again in some of the Key '73 emphases. I decided to try the formula then and went through all the motions of staggered prayer meetings. We met in homes, had round-the-clock prayer, and then an all-night vigil on the Saturday before. Fortunately for me an older layman, a brilliant and devoted Christian, asked me one serious question. After declining to take his turn at three in the morning, he said, "Pastor, do you really believe that the God of our Lord Jesus Christ is going to be impressed or persuaded by my going out at 3:00 A.M.? He knows more about me and my concern for my church than I do. This whole thing takes away from my concept of the nature of God." My honest reaction was one of intense anger, though not expressed, because all the "big name" pastors assured us that they had found the answer to the windows of heaven. The whole thing was a flop and I, at my turn, also fell asleep at the switch. I never tried it again.

My old friend drove home a significant point about prayer. One can't set up Christian prayer routines without first having Christian concepts of the nature of his God. I am not opposed to lengthened prayer meetings be they all night or longer! At times they have the good effect of sensitizing people. However, we must be quite careful lest we give the impression of needing to sensitize God. Much of this all-night business represents such thinking and is simply pagan. One of the great differences in Christian and pagan praying pertains to the party who is to be sensitized to the problem. By sensitized I mean to be made aware and in sympathy with the problem. In the heathen world, God had to be sensitized. Jesus made it clear that man needs sensitization, certainly not the Heavenly Father.

Pagans also assumed that their god was capricious and that one had to be on good terms with the priesthood just in case one needed them. The carry-over into the church is known by all students of church history. Pagans had their priests set aside for the purpose of having them available upon call. These pagan priests were close to the "god-button" and having access to it could act upon request. The Roman Church used the same system in medieval Europe to a fare-you-well. Prayer was the sole property of the priests, and one dared not be on the outs with the priest or the institution he represented. The Catholic Church today has corrected this pagan carry-over to some extent.

It remains the dominant theme in some quarters. The office of the minister has always been precarious in consequence of the loaded meanings attendant to it. Many persons have capitalized on ambiguity, passing themselves off as having some special relationship to God. By being related in some manner to them one can push the god-button. A good example is the use of prayer cloths prayed over by so-called holy men or holy women. What is more up-to-date and sophisticated are the so-called prayer requests sent in to ministers. This "every-one-is-prayed-over-by-me, (or a specially trained group of letter-openers)" routine is nothing more than a reincarnation of the old pagan notion of the elite priesthood. National television carries this Christianized paganism into the homes of millions every week. The aura of a pagan medicine man suggests that if you will place your hands on the television cabinet or radio, power will be transmitted from the station to you. Even more astounding is that most of these programs are taped, meaning that the power must be in a suspended state of invisibility until the tape is aired.

Another pagan notion which is Christianized is the gods' delight in public demonstrations by mortals. Ritual dances and orgies of all kinds finally induced the pagan god to say: "Enough. I am wearied with all this hullabaloo; I will grant your desire." The custom would not be so bad if it were not still around. Recently I read a letter in one of my denomination's magazines demanding that ministers get back to the function of spiritual quests. The letter-writer said he had once witnessed a group of ministers leading a town in a public prayer meeting for rain and it rained. This was part of the "spiritual" dimension to which he wanted a return.

I immediately thought of the time in the Mississippi Delta years ago when the land was gasping for water. A group of wealthy farmers contacted a notable "rainmaker." They obviously didn't trust us ministers of the area. This old boy came down and set up quarters in a field. His presence aroused a great deal of excitement. It was a long hot summer, and we were starving for entertainment to take our minds off the heat. This fellow liked his liquor. So he and a few of the fellows with similar thirsts really tied one on, as they described it. They danced like crazy men around the fire which was sending chemicals up into the heavens. You will never believe it, but it rained like mad the next day. In fact, it rained so hard in one place that some fields were flooded and the fellows who owned that section thought the whole thing was a bit overdone. They were mad at God, the drunks, the chemicals, and anyone else responsible!

My point is that I believe a group of ministers praying for rain makes about as much sense as my drunk friend. What is the difference? The object of the petition is God and the subject is rain. If rain is what one is after isn't one method about as good as the next? Praying for rain is based on some of the agricultural promises of God's help in the Old Testament. Jesus corrected these himself by saying that it rains on the just and unjust and the sun shines in the same way. Praying for rain assumes that the need is seen by men more clearly than by God and that a public demonstration in the town square might get God's attention so he could answer their pleas. A minister on a platform in the town square praying for rain does not put us in the best Christian perspective, it seems to me.

Pagan praying resorted to gimmicks to influence their gods. They looked upon man's misfortunes as the judgment of the gods. When misfortune came, one was out of gimmicks. A Christian does not interpret misfortune as a direct punishment from God. As illustration I call to attention some of the sermons on tithing or giving. I have before me now a pamphlet from a large religious concern. It states that material

67

prosperity and the absence of misfortune come to those who take God at his word. When certain conditions are met, God is bound.

We have heard the testimony that "I promised God I would tithe if he would grant me this. He did and I have lived up to my word." The thought follows that one will be cursed if he withholds the tithe. On the other side of the coin are the many who have tithed who never demanded such return. Many who have not been made rich materially have remained faithful to the Lord.

But there is a lot of pagan superstition still around. A St. Christopher medal or a Bible on the dashboard of a car is nothing more than an approach to God on the gimmick level. We cannot ever, as Christians, pray with the idea in mind that we deserve or merit anything. At no time can we ever put God in a corner. The Christian lives by faith, not by meritorious deeds. Our God is not a good luck charm.

I would like to mention one other pagan notion which we carry with us today. It is the notion of "signing off" the moment prayer is over. Pagans had separate hours and times for prayers. I never have favored presidential days of prayer and the prayer-breakfast scene sounds more like breakfast than prayer to me. In fact I have ignored such occasions. It seems to me that suddenly proclaiming a day of prayer is closely related to the pagan notion that the gods get lonely, and people ought to go visit them. National days of prayer sound as if we are saying, "All right, everyone, let's all stop and tell the good Lord that we haven't forgotten him." A group of youth recently stopped in their service to "give God a hand." Since they had thanked all their other sponsors it was suggested that the Big Man in the Sky ought to get his share. I hope not all of them were on this frequency.

The Christian doesn't see God as sitting next to a telephone awaiting our call, either collectively as a nation or as individuals. The Christian prays in a relationship of *continuing communication*, not with a signing-off-for-now idea until God hears us ring his number. It should be apparent that some of the popular models for praying in the name of Christianity are a long way from gentle Jesus. Much of the time we are posturing at the superstitious shrines of paganism. Somehow, we have not asked Jesus to teach us to pray.

Georgia Harkness has shown us the real tragedy which results from all of this. She says, "There is no way of knowing how many people have given up the practice of prayer because it seemed to them hokum—in plain language 'the bunk'—but the number must run into many millions."

I have not meant to be overly critical or negative. My concern comes after twenty years in the pastorate.

Christians would benefit from the healthy adversary relationship exemplified by lawyers. Opposing lawyers seek without malice to check the credibility of each other. This is my concern—that ideas which are to many of us pre-Christian need to be analyzed. The purpose of analysis is not to hurt people who practice these popularized forms of prayer, but to help others pray who cannot abide the premises of that **prayer. Over the years, having cataloged in my mind** the observations mentioned here, I find myself ashamed, as a pastor, for poor leadership in this area. What is frightening to me, however, is that many persons molding thoughts on prayer today are lacking in theological depth. I hope the church will do some serious thinking about our Lord, the proper concept of the Father, and prayer.

The most pagan concept of God we have witnessed in our time is that of the reluctant heavenly healer —the God who has special people designated to see that healing takes place in the name of Jesus.

III
THE FAITH HEALING SYNDROME

It was only at the beginning of the present century that the recognition prevailed that Gnosticism does not represent a Christian heresy but an independent "pagan" religion which could appear as a Christian heresy only through its penetration into Christian circles and its association with Christian thought-material, as in the same way it appeared as Jewish, Iranian, or Islamic heresy, among others.
—WALTER SCHMITHALS

It happened again—the insanity of withholding medicine from those who need it for the continuation of life. It has happened in my lifetime many, many times. Fortunately, people with better sense usually intervene and persuade the faith healing proponents to allow medicine to be used. In those cases lives are saved, usually in the last stages of allotted time. The great majority of these cases involve a parent who chooses to express his personal faith-healing mind-set through one of his little ones. Little ones go on being sacrificed at the altar of parents' devotion to so-called miracle healing.

The Associated Press writer put it unforgettably.

In the morning, the handsome brown-haired youngster emerged from the bathroom, his head bowed.

"He had a crest-fallen look on his face," Parker remembers, "and he went into the kitchen to prepare his insulin. He came to me with the needle in his hand . . . . I looked at him and I said, 'Wesley, this is a lie of Satan.'" [The lad did not know it but in three days he would be dead.]

"His face broke into a big smile and he watched while I squirted the insulin into the trash can, broke the needle in half and threw it away."

In the last hours of Wesley's coma, his father and mother—who had prayed over him with friends and members of the Assembly of God Church—resisted inclinations to rush out and buy some insulin. Parker said he suddenly knew that the diabetes was caused by "two demons" and "we could no longer give insulin without inviting the demons back."

Wesley was an eleven-year-old child in Barstow, California, and the "Parker" of the story was his father. Later Wesley's parents (who expected him to rise in four days) were charged with manslaughter. The faith-healing traveling evangelist had skipped town and could not be found. As if his evasion were not enough, one national wire service revealed the most remarkable contradiction of terms I have ever read concerning this sort of thing.

The Reverend William H. Robertson, district superintendent of the Assemblies of God churches, said his church "believes in divine healing," but it does not "endorse or condone the throwing away of life-saving medication merely because the individual is presumed healed."

Robertson said, "We do not identify with those who take extreme positions of failing to follow a common sense way of life and would not feel that an extreme position in this regard brings any particular glory to God, nor does it reflect to the credit of the church."

Of course, the most common evasion after the failure of a cure is to say, "They just didn't have the faith, it was not the preacher's fault." Superintendent Robertson uses such words as "extreme position" and "common sense." My suspicion is that the common sense way was not advocated in the services. I have been to many such services before coming to my present conclusion and conviction. I attended a service of this nature twenty-five years ago. A famous faith healer used anything but "common sense" then. He threw crutches away, and while people crawled to get them he would say, "You don't have the faith!" He died suddenly of a crippling disease a few months after I saw him.

Little Wesley is dead, and there will be other little Wesleys who will die as a result of this same madness. All the pious statements preachers can make (Wesley's pastor got frightened when he went into a coma and urged the use of medicine) can't bring the boy back. What is worse, all the valiant efforts of good men to develop an effective insulin treatment have been thrown away.

The fact that we can't eradicate this horror is an

indictment on the church today. Several reasons account for the failure of men to speak out against the "art" of faith healing. Probably the foremost is the American worship of the god of success. This god called Pragmatus is the most powerful force keeping men quiet. Pragmatic means "if it works it is right." Faith healers, by their ability to attract crowds on the one hand and amass fortunes on the other, appear to be successes. This indicates to some that what they are doing is surely of God, or they would not be so successful. We don't criticize success much; in fact we justify it by absurd rationalization.

The second reason the major denominations have stayed neutral is that a segment of all these denominations is involved in these healing services. We hear of Episcopal, Presbyterian, Methodist, and Baptist charismatic healers, as well as nondenominational men of every ilk imaginable. We have had the fringe healers with us for years. However, rather than the larger denominations' being able to come to grips with faith healing on the fringes and meet it at the theological level, the tendency has been to join in. This is so frightening it becomes paralyzing.

Another reason we shy away from submitting this business to a tough critique is an unfounded, spooky notion that to criticize faith healing would be to sin against the Holy Spirit and "grieve" him.

One real reason for avoiding conflict is that this

nation has witnessed the unusual success of Oral Roberts and Kathryn Kuhlman. They have popularized faith healing, made it palatable, given it momentum, and garnered a following. I do not deny that they probably help many people. But we can never be sure how many people are hurt by them. Their popularity indicates to the struggling Christian living with physical pain or mental stress that he doesn't have enough faith to overcome his problems. They do not leave the suffering ones many options. Their logic is hard-hitting and crude. It goes like this. God does not want you to suffer. He wants to heal everyone. And, if you have faith you can get this favor from God. If you are not healed, it is obvious that the fault is yours. The resultant depression is something the pastor sees quite often. While writing these words I was called upon to work with a loving family and a concerned Christian doctor. We all went through the final days of terminal illness with a fine young woman. We had to deal with the problem of faith. She believed that if she had enough faith, she would be healed. We finally communicated to her that God loved her and was with her. After a battle with the implications of faith healing she could finally die in peace. She did not need the theological frustration the healers caused. I could not pray that she would get well. That would have done her more harm than good. She eventually came to realize this.

If the faith healers would treat their work as an option Christians can reject, they would find greater credibility. However, the distinct impression they give is that their brand of healing is the highroad of Christian fidelity. The rest of us who use doctors and medicine are second-class in our ability to trust in God. If the faith healers would approach healing from the standpoint of "if God wills," making this the hinge from which they operate, the problem would be lessened. By making the operative principle an indefinable quality called faith and by making it originate within the sick person, the healers cause real religious problems and tensions. The sick person focuses on his inability to work up enough faith. He may die believing he is a failure doomed by lack of faith. Faith healers back their logic by proof-texting of scriptures. They infer that the true child of God must travel this road. It is at this point that we must challenge their position.

I know they maintain that their healing is not for everyone. But it is difficult to accept their charity when we listen carefully to the full sweep of their message. It is not God's design which limits the effects of their healing. Failure to get well, according to their logic, points directly to the limited faith of the sufferers. For this reason their healing is not for everyone. This attitude unfairly pushes the sick and their families into corners. The resulting frustration causes parents to withhold medicine. They want so badly to show God that they have faith. Like Abraham with Isaac, they dare to take the lives of their own loved one to show that faith. Sadly enough, because we should know better, God does not still the hand with the knife in it today.

Where does faith healing put modern medicine? It would eventually rule out all the courageous work of men and women who have labored long to find cures. It implies that God would really like to have cures come like lightning bolts triggered by a feeling called faith. I am convinced that God has worked through, not against, medicial enterprises. The viewpoint of the faith healers leads to two bad conclusions. If healing does not come about, the lower road to travel is a resort to medicine, after "faith" has failed. Secondly, faith healing poses as a rival to medicine. It pits religion against medicine, when in reality they should work together. Seeing the famous faith healers on television and hearing others ranting on radio late in the night, I'm convinced they all arrive at this same point.

Many of us are intrigued by Oral Roberts' changing public image. When I used to see him in tents he was focusing on healing, and the lines were long. Now that he is on national television in prime time he evinces very little of the healing emphasis, and there are no long lines. He has moved to rambling talks about freeing the spirit. My question is this. If his earlier "healer" role was important then, as he says it was, why not use it for God's glory more so now that he has so much more money and effective means? With all the respect due to him, it does appear that he is abandoning this earlier role without making the break dramatic or telling us why. Mr. Roberts' prime-time efforts have become a syncretism dressed like show biz entertainment, a syrupy mixture of clichés.

The message of the faith healers, whether they stand on balconies in long flowing robes or on lavish television production sets, needs to be carefully analyzed. The incredible logic they espouse is difficult to practice, even if it were true. It follows a carefully cataloged scheme of assumptions to which devotees must ascribe.

Faith healing as an art is either valid or invalid. If it is valid, it should be encouraged. If it is invalid, it should be seen for what it is. In either event, neutrality is less than honest. Many of us who ride in neutral could be guilty of the deaths and emotionally twisted lives faith healing can cause. We wish to be tolerant, but while we are being tolerant many conscientious people are being swayed by its so-called success. One of the saddest reflections on the church today is that it is the secular press which is exposing the falsities of faith healing. The news media is doing more to lead Christians out of the morass than silent church editorials and silent pulpits.

I really think that one of the reasons for silence is that we still live in an age where people are fearful of interpreting the Bible other than literally. Those persons who throw around the faith-healing proof texts or scriptural justification for the "gift" of healing frighten us with their "credentials." It is amazing that many Christians are still gullible about this. Now that Mr. Roberts has moved out of a tent and is speaking with an aura of intellectual backing, serious disagreement is further discouraged. The answer is not malice toward these people. Many of us would like to answer them with sound biblical scholarship. We must accept the challenge and present a better way. For too long this type of selective proof-texting has been ignored. We thought it would go away. Now the lines are drawn and many lay persons are yearning for other options. Yet they do not want to feel they are deniers of their faith. If the use of the Bible in this manner is wrong, it is time for men to say so. If it is right, then we should join these people as soon as possible and take the Bible uncritically. More is at stake than we dared think possible.

With the coming of the book and movie *The Exorcist*, the church is beginning to pay for her sins against good biblical interpretation. The story, purportedly based on fact, tells of a twelve-year-old girl possessed by demons. The demons are, by definition, an outside force which has captured her faculties

79

against her will. Satan speaks blasphemies through her lips. A priest is brought in to drive the demons out.

While our schools of theological education have told us that an uncritical acceptance of biblical models is dangerous, their warning has, in the main, been ignored. The end is not yet in sight, and I fear a resurgence of literal interpretation is just beginning. Sadly enough, many ministers, though trained to use the tools of sound biblical interpretation, have been cowed by the "you-better-take-the-Bible-literally-or-you-will-be-fired" attitude.

Now the old medieval theology of demons is with us again. It is ironic that the Roman Catholic Church has renounced this dark-ages approach, though some Catholics are trying to revive it. What is worse to me is that some Protestants are embracing it. The best way to exorcise demons is to renounce the idea that they exist. Demons never hurt anyone who did not accept their reality.

A church which is unwilling to admit that demons don't exist must come forth with a way to get rid of them when they appear. It is difficult to know what Jesus really believed about the reality of demons. The demented man of the Gerasenes (Mark 5) lost his demons to some swine which drowned in their confusion. Townspeople who had been fearful could now be at ease, because they believed that the demons

80

were drowned. However, it is impossible to drown a spirit—if that spirit really exists. I think Jesus may have been accommodating himself to their views in order to relieve their fears. Demons were to those people outward forces which controlled the will. This belief is as contrary to biblical theology of free will as can be. When the New Testament was written, any disease or malady which could not be explained satisfactorily was labeled a by-product of evil. The necessity of exorcism is usually based on a most unreliable passage in the last few verses of Mark. I am one who does not believe these are genuine words from our Lord in view of the manuscript problems. The words are not found in the older manuscripts as footnotes of more accurate translations indicate. With the revived interest in the occult it is only natural that people would go here for proof texts. But without adhering to the tools of good biblical interpretation one can open a Pandora's box of trouble.

Just as some of the Old Testament references to God are dated, some of the New Testament models of spiritual experience are of no value to modern man. If we attempt to match our experience with the descriptions of first-century experience, without benefit of sound guidelines, we are open to all sorts of spiritual trauma.

The film in question deals with evil in the crudest manner. In so doing it becomes exploitative. I have seen people act terribly irrational when they set out to take the Bible literally. The power of suggestion at work in the uncritical atmosphere and a face-value acceptance of the Bible can do much harm. If this is not a true statement we ought to do away with theological education. Otherwise we should embrace it, for it can lead us out of the morass. We can, however, expect the defection of certain people.

I am not overly concerned about the defection of those who believe in these ancient models. I am greatly concerned about the vast majority of stable individuals who make up our congregations. When an uncritical acceptance of the entire gamut of medieval attitudes enters a church's life, problems grow. Rational people are turned off. When a fringe-type zaniness becomes central, the church can no longer minister to the majority of her members.

I do not blame the father or mother of the little boy I described earlier. I blame reticence on the part of those of us who know better but are quiet. The boy's spiritual leaders who should have known better must share greatly in the guilt. His misled father was only doing as he had been taught to believe—that he should have faith and demonstrate it. He was asked to subscribe to an interpretation of the Bible more primitive than that implied by Martin Luther's act of throwing an inkwell at Satan who had walked into his study.

Let us get to the heart of the faith-healing business by exploring its credentials. The faith healers steadfastly deny that they are healers, but they don't convince many people. Miss Kuhlman told *Christianity Today:*

I resent very much being called a faith healer, because I am not the healer. I have no healing virtue. I have no healing power. I have never healed anyone. I am absolutely dependent upon the power of the Holy Spirit. When I see a sick child, in a moment like that I sense in a special way how dependent I really am. And it's just like that.

If this is true why can't the sick child be healed at home? Why must the sick be brought to special "healers"? The answer is obvious. The healers make it very clear that although it is God who does the healing, it takes place under the sound of *their* voices or at the touch of *their* hands. They talk about their dependence on God, but they promote dependence of the folks beneath the platforms on *them*. The truth of the matter is that these people sell themselves as healers. Since the healing can't take place until they come to town (or until you go to them), for all practical purposes they are practitioners of healing.

The entire faith-healing ministry finds its direction and mandate from *one* lone verse. It is I Corinthians 12:9 where Paul mentions the "gifts of healing." Without I Corinthians, much of this business would have a difficult time finding reasons for its origins. Since the neo-charismatic movement tries to "bring life" to the church (and I am not convinced that it is dead), it is ironic that their inspiration is Corinthians. Of all of the early churches, the one at Corinth was racked with more heresies, more divisions, more sexual and moral degradation and fundamental error than any other early Christian community. In fact, Corinth was probably off-track in more ways than all the other churches put together. To follow the pattern of a Corinthian description of spiritual experience is historical folly. I don't think Paul's advice would be to emulate that experience.

I recommend for serious reading *Gnosticism in Corinth* by Walter Schmithals. Abingdon Press offers a translation of the German work by the brilliant Southern Baptist linguist, John E. Steely. Schmithals' statement, used for the epigraph of this chapter, points to the real problem at Corinth. It was Gnosticism, a system of thought which surfaced all over the first-century world. In every religion where it surfaced, its adherents sought to influence that religion with Gnostic principles. Today many sincere Christians unconsciously operate on Gnostic premises.

Although Gnosticism had many expressions, it can be summed up in one idea here. The body is basically evil because it is matter, flesh and blood. The spirit of man is good but is caged inside this hostile body. The spirit (soul) in man can prove the reality of its union with God only when the evil body is conquered. Man's spirit will then express itself in an extraordinary way. For example, instead of words which can be understood by others, the freed spirit speaks a language with man's tongue which is not even understood by the speaker. Ecstatic expression and abnormal experiences proved one's union with God according to Gnosticism. Many sincere Christians have subscribed to this premise, barking like dogs, jerking, shaking uncontrollably, writhing like snakes, and exhibiting a myriad of other emotionally based antics. Jesus gave no support to such notions.

Lay persons can grasp the Gnostic idea if it is thought of as a war between the body of man and his spirit. When the good spirit becomes one with God's Spirit, the battle is won over the evil body. The writer of Genesis refutes this idea. After making man, God assessed the entire product as good. Any tendency to separate one part of us as good and another part as bad is to lean toward Gnosticism. Sometimes I hear people say, "I got up to speak and God touched my tongue. I spoke for fifty minutes and don't remember a word I said. It was God who spoke through me." For these people, to be led by the Spirit means to be numbed in the mind. It may sound "spiritual," but the assumptions behind it are contrary to sound biblical understanding. All young preachers have at one time or another "leaned" on the Spirit in such extemporaneous moments. I did, and it was terrifying. Persuaded by some sincere people that God would touch my tongue when I got up, I went into the pulpit unprepared. After a brief introduction of my intended remarks, I went blank. Sheer terror seized me, and I can honestly say I don't remember what I said for those fifteen minutes. I am sure it was well-cataloged clichés. I distinctly remember praying while I was talking. My quite rational prayer was, "Dear God, if you will get me through this, I will never come unprepared again." It wasn't the Spirit which had me in his grasp—it was sheer fright.

If God made us to be in control of ourselves, it does him no service, nor does it prove our spirituality, when we act irrationally. I would rather believe that to be filled with the Spirit is to be rational and in control. It doesn't make much sense that God has given man such a marvelous thing as the mind and then, in order to prove that he is in union with God, he should be asked to go out of his head. The Corinthians made the error of accepting Gnosticism. Similar error is made today. Paradoxically, the error at Corinth is called Christian by some today.

This discussion can help us understand the faith-healing syndrome. In that context demons cause the body to be ill; illness is of the devil. Christianized Gnosticism maintained that physical pain was the penalty one paid for not being set free by God's Spirit. Thus, the only way to measure one's union with God was to be free from pain. Once again sick people are exploited by this logic. It is damaging to normal healing processes. The frame of one's mind is closely tied to the healing of the body. Doctors can isolate the cause of illness in terms of science, but it works against healing when the patient is convinced his illness stems from his lack of spiritual vitality. The sick are often gullible, while almost powerless to work up a release of their spirits to "reach out to God."

Paul never was more frustrated with a group of Christians than with the Corinthians. He wrote to them in an effort to help them reconcile the differences which divided them into hostile camps. Schmithals believes that he was primarily interested in restoring their fellowship. We might wish that he had challenged their views as he did in the Colossian Letter. Paul obviously sees their drift toward the Gnostic notions but refrains from debate.

His assertion that he can do anything they can do suggests his reluctance to argue. However, it is clear he is not sold on what they are doing. Although he says he too could babble in an unknown tongue, he maintains that he will stick to words he can understand. I am convinced that the inordinate desire for experiencing ecstasy and an irrational freeing of one's spirit borders on Gnosticism. I am also convinced that

Paul realized it but that his main concern was to restore Corinthian fellowship. His random mention of all these ecstatic manifestations was to show the Corinthians he knew what was going on. I do not believe he meant to endorse those actions.

For example, Paul alludes to the practice of baptizing for the dead (I Cor. 15:29). He does not counsel it, practice it himself, or endorse it. Therefore, his description of these practices does not make them authentic either in his mind or as models for us to follow. Paul does not encourage any of these practices with any degree of enthusiasm. And it should be pointed out that those people who endorse a biblical literalism on the "gifts" issue do not practice baptism for the dead.

When he mentions the "gifts of healing," he is offering nothing more than a rambling description of the diverse nature of the ways he has seen the Holy Spirit work. He does not elaborate on any of the characteristics he mentions. In fact, he does not imply that any of these manifestations become callings. He closes with the statement that the Spirit puts into operation, distributing each one as he wills.

Close reading of the passage gives our present question perspective in two ways. In the first place, Paul is merely listing ways he has seen God work in the lives of different people. He does not divide these people into ministries of tongues, ministries of healing, ministries of miracles, ministries of knowledge, etc. Today we don't see these broken up into separate ministries except the healer syndrome. This in itself suggests interesting observations, not the least of which is that the healer role is the only one that can support itself materially. Do traveling ministers come to town advertising themselves as "tongues" evangelists? Would a fellow with the gift of tongues start out to lead from beginning to end a service of babbling? The answer is no—we never heard of such. Yet, this passage can be interpreted to mean this, just as it used to validate the healer role. Furthermore, are elaborate foundations (such as the Kuhlman one) or other organizations based on these other gifts? After all, the same proof-text passage can justify any of these "ministries." But who would go out to a stadium or an auditorium to hear a man merely practice his gift of tongue interpretation, even though he is interpreting heavenly ideas? Imagine a man coming one week who would use the gift of tongues and the next week his being followed up by a week-long ministry by an interpreter of the tongues spoken the week before. Of course, that would be absurd, but the same scripture can be utilized to give as much credence to these and other "callings" as to the faith healers.

Or what about an evangelistic organization based on that other gift—the gift of wisdom? Do we hear of a ministry based on a person's coming with his crusade of wisdom? By wisdom we mean whatever Paul meant and of that we are uncertain. After all, "to one is given the gift of wisdom," says Paul in the same passage. Or here is one that is sure to be a loser in the field of "ministry gifts." That is the "gift of faith." Now there is a stopper! What on earth did Paul mean by this gift? Is it a type of faith that others do not have? If you could see it demonstrated what would this gift look like? Just imagine seeing the billboard ad forecasting the arrival in our town of a man with his "ministry of faith." That buildup alone wouldn't draw enough people to attract mosquitoes. Yet, each of the so-called separate and distinct gifts is as scriptural as the gifts of faith healing.

The second thing a closer look at the passage reveals is that what Paul described is not at all the same phenomenon we see today. He gives no indication that one gift is more important than any other. The key to the entire passage Paul gives himself in the closing statement. He says the Spirit puts all of these gifts into operation as he chooses. The gifts are fluid and may be seen from time to time in people only as God chooses. Nowhere does he ascribe a separate ministry to any individual for a lifetime or any specific period of time. It is not that certain men have the ability to use the gifts, but rather that the Spirit uses certain men as instruments to demonstrate the gifts. "Gift" demonstrations are subject to no human plan, but are part of the mystery of the Spirit's own will.

Considering this evidence, it is difficult to see any authority whatsoever for the development of a professional calling based on any one of the lines of thought Paul drops in this passage. In the mystery of God's actions one man might play a role in a healing miracle (perhaps as a Christian doctor) one time in his life and never again! Or, some men might possess several of these characteristics for a specific purpose and never be used of the Holy Spirit again in the same way. It is significant that Paul uses the plural "gifts of healing" while of the other distinctions he says "gift." People are healed by the Spirit in many ways. Paul did not stereotype healing as the healing crusades do.

The proof-texters really don't have a text, at least not this one, to offer as biblical warrant for the professional healer role. I am under no illusion that these sincere people will agree with me. I do hope to show to others who do not agree with them that there is a viable option. Paul said that the Holy Spirit will give the gifts of healing to a person and put them into operation only as he (the Holy Spirit) chooses. It is a manifest violation of this passage to pass oneself off as being in a position to be "used of God" in a healing campaign. How does the healer know that the Holy Spirit will work through him on that occasion? Yet, healers enter into their services with this assumption. Instead of focusing on the Spirit's willingness or unwillingness to heal, they focus on the ability or the inability of people to produce faith. The healers (and some of the other charismatics) actually violate the passage they use to justify their role. They emphasize that folks ought not to "quench the Spirit." According to this passage it is they who are quenching the Spirit! Anytime a man attempts to computerize the activities of the Holy Spirit, it is he who is quenching the Spirit. To advertise a great healing service and have folks come to see the Holy Spirit being put into operation is near blasphemy. According to this passage, the Holy Spirit might not choose to operate on the night of the big event. Even if he does he might not heal everyone present. Sufferers who go away without healing are not told that the Spirit has arbitrarily left them out. They are told that the trouble springs from their own faithlessness. Invariably the assumption is stated loudly at such a service that it is God's will that healing, tongues, etc., occur and will happen only upon a clear exercise of faith. That assumption may be sincere but is without scriptural warrant. No man can (according to this scripture) ever guarantee any of these gifts on any given occasion. They are set in operation only as the Spirit chooses.

The healers I've seen, from the world famous ones to the wild-eyed ones in hysterical, small-town revivals, justify their services all on the gift they have from the Spirit. This passage says that if they had it, they wouldn't have it for long—only as the Spirit decides. Certainly, it can't be bottled, soaked into prayer cloths, or transmitted through radio and television sets. The typical approach is that we Christians are to pray for what is called "the baptism of the Spirit." It is referred to as a one-time experience. But Paul does not see union with the Spirit as the result of any one exercise or experience. He views the Spirit's use of these gifts as a phenomenon which comes and goes according to the Divine will. I think that a great injustice is done to Scripture when men interpret being "filled with the Spirit" as reaching the ultimate plateau.

Being baptized with the Holy Spirit is synonymous with being used of the Spirit or with possessing gifts as seen in this passage. There is no guarantee that this state is permanent or that it can be demonstrated as we choose. The "now-I've-got-it, watch-me-use-it" routine certainly does not find its roots in Pauline thought. I believe in being filled with the Spirit and being baptized with the Spirit. However, I believe that it is never a one-time experience and certainly not something that one can manipulate because one has been blessed by it in the past. The entire emphasis of the new charismatics is a reversal of Pauline thought.

Paul believed in healing of a miraculous manner

and so do I. However, these things take place as they did in his life in the most unexpected places. They were never planned in advance. It is time that many sincere people, who also believe the Bible, quit allowing themselves to feel less than Spirit-led because they do not subscribe to a misinterpretation of the I Corinthians passage. I am certain that a case can be made from scripture against a professional ministry which isolates the gifts of the Spirit. Nowhere does the Bible teach that we can put God on trial and manipulate him in any observable routine. When real miracles happen, the mystery of the timing is just as elusive as the fact that a miracle has occurred. I do believe in being used of the Spirit. But it is impossible to predict the time or situation where the Spirit will use us.

So, I do believe in miraculous healing. I've seen it take place. However, it must be said as frankly as possible—I don't know *why* or *how* it came about! For God to remain God, he must do his work of this nature in his own way. If we could, by prayer cloths, oil, and certain men or women, induce him to reveal the chemistry of miracles, he would no longer be God. We would then become as gods and he would be reduced to a giant computer. Upon going through a routine or ritual we could predict the result. That would be infinitely wrong. Never was a church a greater embarrassment to true Christian religion than the Corinthians were, and Paul spent his energy appealing to them to act rationally. It is an ironic refutation of the intent of the Letters to Corinth when the present charismatic movement begs men to psych themselves into a state of ecstasy and then to offer this as proof of union with God. Yet, this is their main thrust!

Before we go further, one word of pastoral advice. Don't be led to give testimony of how you were miraculously healed if that has been your experience. God doesn't need the credit. Someone listening to you may be as committed a Christian as you are. He may be incurably ill. One day you had a remission of your disease, but he didn't. If you speak of your experience even to give God the glory, a crisis of faith is produced in a suffering one whom God loves as much as he does you.

A leading religion editor of a midwest newspaper interviewed me one day about this kind of situation. She said that her grandmother went to a healing crusade and wept bitter tears in faith that her invalid condition might be removed. It was not, and she worried to her dying day about why God didn't choose to love her enough to ease her pain. Every time she heard a testimony she was pushed down a little bit more. I stopped having this kind of testimony in my churches many years ago for this very reason. God doesn't need the publicity, and this kind of testimony has a tendency to make exceptional spiritual experiences seem commonplace. Spiritual experiences are not all alike. Paul makes that abundantly clear.

If there is any historical basis for testimonies it would be in the Gospel of John in which various testimonies are given. These testimonies basically affirm that Jesus, as Christ, is the Son of God. I would like to offer some views on what is rapidly becoming an unfortunate stereotyping of the personal testimony. For twenty-five years I've been interested in the form of public testimonies. I used to hear the Old Fashioned Revival Hour with Charles E. Fuller. His wife would always read a shared experience from some letter-writer. As I reflect upon that manner of testimony, I also remember the simple extemporaneous words of people in churches. I think there is a great difference in the healthy approach of those days and the canned artistry now before us. In fact, we are seeing the popularization of a banquet-type testimonial. When this is used as the major focus of testimonials, they often become sheer entertainment.

I have observed that there are at least three recognizable categories into which the traveling testimony-givers fall. The first is what I would call, "from darkness to light." The second one can be called, "from light to greater light," and the third, "from greater light to the full light.", When you hear a present-day testifier, see if he or she does not fall into one of these categories. If you follow these people for any length of time you will be amazed to observe that they will have moved through each stage. In the first stage the testimony relates one's lost condition. At this point the emphasis is upon God's power in salvation. With good theological understanding this level is healthy. However, for these people this theme will not endure for long. After awhile it becomes dull, even to the testifier. The person begins to need a greater emotional experience, and it is not unusual to hear him say, "I was a Christian for many years, but I really didn't know what it was like to truly give myself to the Lord." Here we have the light-to-greater-light category. This level is seen in the autobiographies of celebrities and others who want to share with us. The person will get mileage out of this level for a period of time, and then it too, begins to sputter out. He or she then moves to the third category which is expressed something like this: "I thought I had been devoting my life completely to Jesus. But I was shown that I did not possess the power to exhibit the gifts of the spirit-filled life." This is the greater-light-to-the-full-light category.

The third-category testimonies are reserved for the "inner circle" groups. This is the home turf of the new charismatics. Charismatic fellowships are organized at this level. Revived for the benefit of these groups are the visions, ecstatic experiences, and healing. Very soon we will see the common practice of demon exorcism. From this point the person has nowhere to go since the zenith has been reached. Therefore, in order to compensate for the need for greater emotional experience, the testimony-givers become zealots. With great missionary zeal they encourage their listeners, who have gone through stages one and two, to join them in stage three. This becomes the final initiatory rite for being completely God-possessed, and the benefits are what they call, "gifts of the Spirit." There is very little difference in this third category from the pagan mystery religions of the ancient world. It was level three which had been reached by a minority at Corinth.

What we often see taking place in these three levels is an unwillingness on the part of the individual to accept a critical evaluation of his religious experience. The person is blind to the fact of his moving from one level to the next. Without this discipline he or she feeds on the need for greater degrees of emotional satisfaction, much in the same manner as a dope addict. I cannot help but believe that some of the present trend in the testimony cult borders on emotional illness. It seems to be a world away from the healthy statements of praise and assurance that many of the past testimonies used to exhibit. However, the past also saw some of the same.

Unless the church is willing to see much of the charismatic business for what it is, we shall see no

98

end of irrational religion and the return to medieval practices. The worst result will be a retrogression of religious insight. This will most certainly be accompanied by the rejection of Christianity on the part of stable people within our congregations. When such degeneration occurs who can blame them!

Throughout this book I have tried to offer alternatives for Christians who cannot subscribe to some tenets of the contemporary scene. I would like to quote the words of a young minister who has never said these things publicly. In fact he wishes to remain anonymous. He presents an alternative Christian position worth considering.

Having come from a family where I was taught to pray as early as I can remember, and also being a minister—it seemed only natural that in this situation I should pray. I lay in the mud of a yard with rain falling on me. I wanted to pray. However, I could not do so without mixed feelings.

With unbelievable clarity and suddenness a car wreck had just occurred. I was lying on my right side with glass in my head. Later I was to find out that I had a brain concussion. I was experiencing extreme pain in my left leg and ankle which was broken in two places. I also had a dislocation, tendon and ligament tear, glass in my mouth, and pain all over my body. I remember hearing whispers of my being paralyzed. A feeling of fear came over me I had never known before.

From my Christian background it seemed only natural to want to pray that I would be all right and would not die. Yet it seemed cheap to ask something for myself that could not be granted to others. Four young women in the other vehicle were hurt. One was killed, and one was in intensive care for a long time. The young man driving the car I was in had blood all over him from cuts on his face and other injuries. To recall the scene now is eerie.

As I lay on the wet ground with rain coming down, a beautiful elderly lady came out of her home and put a blanket over me. She held an umbrella over me and in so doing got herself soaking wet. Later I found out that she had just gotten over pneumonia, and her act of love was for a person she did not know.

As she held my hand, I kept thinking of what Bonhoeffer said to a man as they lay on the floor while bombs fell all round the building.

When the man called out "O God, O God," Bonhoeffer couldn't bring himself to offer him any Christian encouragement or comfort. All he could do was glance at his watch and say, "It won't last any more than ten minutes."

All I could think to do was to hang on for ten more minutes. Surely then someone would be there in an ambulance, take me to a hospital, get me medical attention, and the horrible pain would be gone.

Ten minutes grew into an hour. It was fully three hours before I got an injection for the relief of pain. Now, almost a year has past. The pain over the loss of life and the change of my life-style is still with me. And I must say that prayer is still a part of my life.

Prayer to me is a process whereby I affirm pain as a part of life. Sometimes the only comfort is to face it head on with the realization that accepting it does not mean one does not have faith. Instead, one's faith allows one to deal effectively with pain and hurt. Why I lived, and why that fine young woman did not—another child of God as precious as any of

God's children—is a puzzle to me. She had dreams, hopes; she loved and was loved the same as I. I really don't understand it all. I only know that I felt that it was selfish to pray as I lay in that yard when a person lay lifeless. My faith didn't get me out of the excruciating pain. It did help me to hold on.

My spared life and another's death will forever remain a mystery to me. Hitler ordered Bonhoeffer to be hanged. I quote him again as he wrote from his prison cell on the day I was born, September 25, 1943; "What will come out of my time here it is too early to say. But something is bound to come out of it."

If God has done something for you of an unusual and miraculous nature then the quieter you keep it, the better it is for everyone concerned. There are reasons for this other than the possibility of hurting innocent people. Another is that you do not know *how* it came about, so how can it be described? Nor do you know *why* it came about, so be grateful you are alive. You could lead people up alleyways of false hopes only to be hurt beyond description. I cringe at healing testimonies when I hear the old revival cliché "Give God the credit." The finest thing you can do in response to a miracle is to commit yourself in greater discipleship. Our Lord warned those he healed not to spread their news in the community. He sent them to the priests, thus tying them to greater service to God through the channels of organized religion.

How well I remember a day in 1949 when I was

making a home visit with another minister. World War II was still vividly in our minds. During the visit a troubled-looking man admitted that he had not lived up to a miracle-bargain. As he wept softly he told a hair-raising story of being in a foxhole in the midst of seven dead soldiers. The Japanese jumped into the hole and bayoneted each man. He had smeared blood over his face and hidden himself under a dead body. Then he prayed that if God would let him live, he would go back home and serve him. The Japanese missed him with their bayonets. He lay still for over two days until they were out of the area. Then he told us that he forgot his vow, or at least that he didn't live up to it. He said he was willing to come and give his testimony and get right with God. The astute pastor I was with said, "Friend, if you give that kind of testimony, even though it is truly a miracle, how do I explain about the sons of the half-dozen mothers who will hear you, these I have personally buried, who were killed all over the South Pacific?" He then told the man to come and join the church, to keep his story in the chambers of his heart, and to use his energies in committed Christian living. The man joined the church, was faithful for six months and dropped out. How do we explain all of this? *We don't*. Better men than he lost their lives, and it would have been terribly wrong for him to try to pay a debt with his lips that he was unwilling to pay with his life.

Yes, I believe in miracles, healing, and all kinds of supersensory things. Jesus believed in a phenomenal and a supersensory world. However, there is another mystery, God's mystery of timing. His mystery of cause and effect we can't fathom. There will always be this element in the God-man relationship if God is to be God and man is to be man.

Now that we have explored the biblical credentials, we need a closer look at the assumptions of faith healing. It is for all practical purposes an attempt at manipulating God. Praying for the sick is all too often evidence of treating God as if he were better than aspirin or the best antibiotic. For example, one day a lady came to me and said, "Pastor, my husband is in the hospital. He has been there for two days, and we at first didn't think that he was seriously ill. This is why I haven't called on you before. Awhile ago the doctor told me that he has pneumonia and that he is sicker than we thought. He is not responding to the antibiotic as he should, so I thought I better ask you to pray for him." If that had happened only one time in my ministry, I could pass it off. This is like saying that God is a little stronger medicine than penicillin. At first it was doubtful whether *that* strong a medicine (God) would be needed. After it appeared that the prescribed medicine was not going to work, and since at that time there was nothing stronger she sent for the preacher, or the God-manipulator.

103

Before the discovery of penicillin that same lady would have called on God sooner, say, right after the sulfa drug played out. Today she would have waited to call on the "super-medicine" (God) until after she had tried the Mycine and other wonder drugs. God to this woman was a huge mass of super power. She hoped she wouldn't have to tap it, but the sickness was worse than she expected. God became a drug and the minister was the pharmacist.

Man has always tried to manipulate his deities. There are reasons for this. Man, with his capacity for reason, is mystified by his journey through this life. He is not conscious of having come, but he is conscious of going and not coming back. A part of the mystery is the eerie silence of the other world. Man is aware of his finiteness. He knows he can be cut off before he draws his next breath. He lives with the death of his fellows. This prompts a terrible sense of fear. He knows that sickness or that any diminishing of his natural strength could lead to his death. In this sense all sickness is looked upon as being bad. Man has learned to regard sickness as a warning signal.

Man knows that the drive to combat these ills is a part of human progress. The continual quest of medical research is scientific manipulation of the visible material universe. We are always looking for permanent cures for impermanent bodies. Consequently, the manipulation of unseen power lies close to this quest.

If men of science can manipulate the seen to discover ways to prolong life, men of religion should be able to render an equal service by manipulating the powers of the unseen. At least this is the purpose some have seen for religion.

Ancient history is replete with stories of men's lives being spared by the gods. The history of Israel is not without these. The classic example is good King Hezekiah to whom we referred. His life was spared for fifteen additional years (II Kings 20:6). The story of Hezekiah is a mystery of God's will. Although it has opened up hope for similar situations, it cannot be taken as the normative way God works.

Much of the praying Christians perform over sick-beds is void of any spiritual purpose. It is a last resort when medicine fails. Now ironically, since we have better medicine, there is less praying over sickness than in the past. Possibly there will be even less in the future.

The inconsistency in the way we pray for the sick is interesting. Upon closer scrutiny the typical prayer for healing is highly qualified and selective. Yet, if we are going to entreat on all-powerful God, why stop where we stop? For example, we never pray for a hand or leg to suddenly materialize. Never have I been asked for, or have I seen the healers pray for, the miraculous creation of an arm for an amputee. Seldom does anyone pray that eyes will form in empty sockets. We attempt to pray within limitations while we steadfastly claim that we do not. Not many folks pray for an arm to come back as often as they pray for a germ to disappear.

In my experience, prayer meetings called for the purpose of praying for sick people have followed certain predictable patterns. Few, if any, are consistent with higher Christian principles. Usually, a community or church gets excited enough to do such a thing only for notable people, i.e., the good King Hezekiahs. I remember the radiologist's telling me that the dark mass looked exactly like a massive malignancy. He recommended immediate exploratory surgery. As a young man of thirty and minister in a prominent county seat, it was hard to keep this news quiet. In the hours before surgery the desperation of the moments was eased somewhat by the tenderness of family and friends. The chairman of my board came saying he thought that the board would ask each church to pray for me. Our church was to begin a round-the-clock vigil. This note of genuine love really helped. Yet, I quickly recalled an experience of only a year before. Miles from town lived a twenty-eight-year-old mother of two children. She was very, very poor. The doctors went out to make her as comfortable as possible while she lay incurably ill with cancer. I was asked by a doctor to go as often as I could. Few were the times that I had seen suffering like hers.

I remember asking prayer and concern for her at the close of a morning worship service. Until her death a month later, only two ladies from our church went to see her, and then only once. She died in loneliness, in pain, and loved by few. When I officiated at her funeral less than fifty folks were there.

I remarked to my board chairman that it was not fair that that woman had to die in a share-cropper's cabin without the corporate concern of our church while I should somehow merit specially-called prayer meetings. I asked that no such meetings be called. I said that my case rested with God and that there was no need for a public display of feverish frenzy.

It often is the case that when a community is in a stir, wanting God to "come and heal," it is for a notable person. Only God knows how many lonely souls have died without such concern, simply because they were not important enough in the measurement of the world. Is this type of selective praying Christian, or even fair in the secular sense?

The second assumption made in this kind of praying is that God is a third party who is either not concerned or uninformed. The principal party is the sick one; the second party is the representative prayer group; and God comes in third. Is it not true that a gathering for the express purpose of praying for a sick loved one assumes that God is not as concerned as the folks who come together? Men are being put in a

107

better light than God our Father. I have been in prayer meetings where some brother begins by saying, "Now Lord, we are here to pray for our Brother Sam. Lord you know how we need him a little longer." Now if God knows that why are we to tell him so? Never is there a time when we have to inform God about the situation. We need to cease praying for the sick in a way that makes God seem to care less for them than we do.

The Christian doesn't look upon illness as being without purpose and, therefore, completely bad. Jesus was selective in the healing of physical bodies. I cringe when I hear faith healers say that it is never God's intention that man endure any pain. Pain is an effective schoolmaster for greater spiritual growth. Whenever a Christian falls among the sick, the spiritual purpose is always to be kept in focus. When a man or woman becomes a Christian, that person has committed *body* and *soul* to Christ's service. It is a personal identity that is established. Each man has an I.D. card in the Kingdom, and whatever happens to him from then on involves him as a Christian. The Christian doesn't need some healer to call his problem to God's attention. Christ is in heaven interceding for each of his children. We can take our burdens to God directly. God is not impressed by religious superstars. To be a Christian is to live to serve God as a first cause. God comes above all kinds of personal choices we would otherwise have made. The Christian should not approach God in prayer to talk about effect. He should always come to God to talk about cause. The Christian doesn't ask *why* a thing happened—he always *seeks to find good* in the situation. He lives in an atmosphere of first cause, not secondary intervention. When a Christian becomes desperately ill he doesn't begin to pray as if *now* he wishes God would step into the picture. That is secondary intervention. Rather, he believes that in God's mysterious dealings with his children, God can be glorified in the cause. God was directly involved *before* the sickness came. Therefore, the Christian always tries to see purpose within sickness. He is not merely preoccupied with the prospect of being extricated from the situation. We pray that we can work with God in the blessings of illness as God works in us. Healing lines in which the emphasis (regardless of how many times the healers deny it) is strictly on relieving physical suffering needs to rise to a higher level, the level of serving God *through* suffering.

For the Christian, praying for the sick, or praying for anything, is basically predicated upon the principles seen in Jesus' contribution to prayer. The heart of the gospel is not that man has been offered an avenue to an earthly Nirvana, a release from pain. The gospel is not the story of God taking us out of our misery. Relief does come at times, but in mysterious, not cal-

109

culated, ways. The gospel is simply that *God is with us!* The Angel said that His name would be called Emmanuel which means "God with us," with us in pain. When the Christian discovers that Jesus is with him, many of the pagan assumptions we have been exploring are cleared away. Valid Christian praying does not demand miracles. They are unnecessary in the light of the great miracle of God's being here in Jesus Christ, living and dying among men. As our resurrected Lord, he is with us in our trials, and this is all the Christian ever asks for. Men have gone through unbelievable hells in life supported by this knowledge. He cleared up so many things for us that we should continually look to him for direction.

I want to say again that if lawyers can with meticulous scrutiny probe the positions of their fellows in behalf of their clients, why can't this practice be acceptable among Christians? It is in this spirit that I would like to discuss the new charismatics. Emotional experience in religion is on the upswing. The worst result is that many rational people are going to turn the Christian message off. Unfortunately, through their sincere zealousness, many neo-charismatics would like to take over every denomination and local church they can find. They will do it only one way—by quoting proof texts and threatening the rest of Christ's body by implying sin against the Holy Spirit in any objections. This entire movement of prayer language, tongue-babbling, unbridled public demonstrations, healing services, and now demon-exorcism is not new. The last century saw it rack one great denomination—Methodism. From it came division, new sects, and an anti-intellectual, antirational mind-set. It is precisely this frame of mind which is once again rearing its head and quoting the gifts of the Spirit.

A lot is being said today about pluralism. This is a nebulous, undefined term usually intended to mean there is room for every view under the same roof. Only the extremely naive or those who are completely detached from practical experience advocate it without at the same time offering guidelines. There are two things wrong with pluralism as far as the neo-charismatic pentecostals are concerned. One is that they will not practice the same tolerance they wish from others. In some quarters there is screening of books which are opposed to their views. Such policies of resistance to investigation reveal that the charismatics cannot abide a so-called pluralism with those who oppose them—one camp has to give. Much of Protestantism and Catholicism has faced these views several times in history and has rejected them. History has never known a period when the two views have been able to work in harmony for any length of time.

Many charismatics accuse the opposition of renouncing the need to be filled with (or baptized with)

111

the Spirit. The second reason pluralism is impractical is that the obsessive demand for this secondary experience by the charismatics is divisive. It was so at Corinth when it first surfaced in Christian history, and its record is consistent to this very day. It is difficult to find a single instance in which the existence of one of these minority cells has not caused unfortunate circumstances both for them and the majority. Much of the time the attitude of the minority toward the rest of the church borders on self-righteousness since their fellows do not exhibit the gifts of the Spirit, notably tongues-speaking.

The alarming growth of this new Pentacostalism is exemplified by a *NEWSCOPE* report on a United Methodist event in Iowa which drew 2,500 people. "With perhaps a third of the participants numbering themselves among the growing charismatic movement, the Iowa event witnessed a variety of experiences rare for a United Methodist-related gathering: Tongue-speaking, revelation and interpretation of visions, prophecy, and prayers for healing." *Each of these aspects involves the suppression of the rational!*

I would like to endorse an abide-under-the-same-roof attitude, but where these minority views are present there is a record of divisiveness that defies description. Unfortunately we are not dealing with a problem which can be solved with tolerance. We are dealing with a phenomenon which is completely at odds with critical biblical investigation, a psychological overview of man's actions, and restrained emotions at worship. History has seen the creation of an amazingly wonderful place for this phenomenon. It is in the Pentecostal churches. This is the place where the *new* Pentecostals ought to go. It is here that they would find fulfillment. It is here that they would find a home. The surfacing of these ideas in the other denominations can only bring trouble. It always has. They have not brought anything new to church history. Their ideas are as old as Corinth and are practiced every week in Pentecostal churches. There is a home for the new Pentecostals—in the old Pentecostal congregations. Here they can find unanimity.

Who is really at fault in the death of the diabetic child? Or, more properly, what is at fault in the lad's death? Can it be said that Christian principles were followed by his parents? If a drunk driver had hit him, many people would be up in arms who are not so now. The lad is just as dead. Are the principles operating here part of the faith given to us by our Lord Jesus? Or is this business really a revival of pagan Gnosticism, as Schmithals says? The answer is obvious—much of the charismatic revival, unless given wise direction, will revive first-century heresies and become Christianized paganism.

Who or what allowed little Wesley to die—in the name of the Christian religion?

113

IV
JESUS' DISTINCTIVE CONTRIBUTIONS TO PRAYING

If your prayer is answered (but how, you do not know), it is because you have entered into the kingdom of God, today, not by your eventful present, but by the very presence of the Lord of the ages.

—JACQUES ELLOL

Every book I have read on Christian prayer has had a chapter on Jesus, the man of prayer. This is as it should be. My approach to distinctive Christian praying would be greatly lacking if I did not include this chapter. When one begins a study of prayer in the Christian perspective, he eventually comes to a study of our Lord at prayer. I have heard a great deal of emphasis put on the times Jesus prayed. The mechanics of his praying, such as timing and other aspects, do not interest me as much as they once did. These seem to have been an accommodation to his life-style. One really doesn't grasp the power and insight of Jesus' life in prayer through mere emulation

.of his habits. It is altogether possible to be rigorous in the discipline of punctual praying at set times yet really not be praying at all. If prayer is by definition communication with God, there is one particular element of communication we should consider. When one person talks with another at stated times each day—if that is the case—it is possible that on some occasions the communication is not very good. Sometimes there is no communication at all. We all know that there are times when we cannot .communicate well with one another as a result of fatigue, stress, or preoccupation with other matters. This element in the communicative process is important. Therefore, to find comfort because we have set times for prayer, even though it has been recommended by most books on prayer, is to overlook some real aspects of com munication It means finding comfort in form or routine. When a person prays and how he prays is not as important as manuals on prayer sometimes lead us to believe. The old ploy, that if we are not in a routine of prayer, we will not pray, sounds quite logical and trustworthy. It just isn't so! At this point I want to inject a word about pulpit utterances on this and other related aspects of our common faith.

Some time ago I observed a serious flaw in my ministry. At times, in sermons on prayer, witnessing, and other matters related to Christian growth, an unrealistic attitude crops up. We preachers sometimes make the mistake of preaching to our laity as if they were professionals. When a sermon on prayer maintains that one ought to set aside time with God, say a half-hour or so, it is patently unfair to lay persons when compared with the professional minister. The same is true with witnessing. I think of the many wonderful lay persons who work shifts or who get up early to go to work. It is unfair to attempt to legislate routines in their lives which we as ministers can accomplish more easily because of our jobs. I come to my study, and my job offers me the time and environment for reflection, meditation. I visit in behalf of the church as a regular routine. If I had to get up to commute twenty miles through heavy traffic, I wonder if I could find the time to be as disciplined in prayer, witnessing, etc. Too much pulpit admonition is based on a way of life that is routine for professional clergy but is hard to accomplish for the laity. Also, some women overlook the stress their husbands are under. Many of them get the children off to school, and then they have their quiet time with God before tackling the many duties of their day. This is as it should be, but neither they nor the pastor should sit in judgment on "old George" down at the plant who is going through anything but a quiet time of reflection.

The devotional life of the highest quality is all too often glamorized as a role which is easier for some than for others. This kind of devotional experience is easier to accomplish for the pastor, some housewives, or some wealthy laymen who can detach themselves from their jobs without penalty. In fact, some very good men, after they have made their life financially secure, make a hobby out of religion. No judgment is implied here except to say that they need to be aware that their income affords them the peace of mind for prayer times. But the doctor who has been on call all weekend is a different case. He has slept a scant few hours in three days and in the meantime has sewed up a hundred drunks beaten up, cut up, and smashed up in fights, car wrecks—you name it. He would have a difficult task establishing a prayer time. Many good Christian doctors pray during these moments of stress, but there is no pattern to their prayer. Absolutely too much emphasis has been given to a romantic description of the great prayerful Christian. The poor average guy in the pew starts thinking that he just isn't with it because his hectic life doesn't offer these times. But he doesn't have an environment such as a study with a carpeted floor and good books. We ministers have a tendency to describe devotion in categories which are quite unrealistic for the laity. I think about God most of the day because everything in my life communicates this to me. That clerk who deals with disgruntled people eight hours a day just doesn't have the luxury of reflecting on the beautiful blue Galilean Sea that I do. I invite people to church and inquire as to their soul status, because they expect me to do it, and because it is my job. Members of my congregation are in a much more difficult position.

I remember well my seminary days. No place is quite as unrealistic in the respect we are pointing out as the world of theological academics. For the first nine-month term it was God, the Holy Scriptures, Christ, prayer; and on and on our minds went. When summer came, the stress of other needs became more apparent, particularly that very "secular" need for "food" money. I got a job as weigh-master during the wheat harvest. Trucks would line up for over a mile during my twelve-hour shift. This went on six days a week for two months. I learned an important lesson all ministers and teachers need to keep on learning! I was amazed at how little I thought about God during those days. The environment of dust, dirt, truck noises, and impatient truck drivers was something slightly different from the classroom then or my study now. Somehow Calvin's Institutes lost their significance in the sweat of that summer. We are hearing a lot about sabbaticals for teachers and pastors. They are usually leaves for study. A year as a department-store clerk would be much a better aid in preparing us to interpret the Christian life for our people.

Having said this, it is easier for me to say that *any* Christian can more easily come to grasp Jesus' understanding of prayer if he will get his eyes off the mechanics of prayer. I am far more interested in Jesus' basic assumptions about prayer than the manner in which Jesus prayed. If we can grasp how Jesus thought we can better understand how Jesus prayed.

In the Sermon on the Mount Jesus laid down the basis for Christian praying in a striking passage.

And when you pray, you must not be like the hypocrites; for they love to stand and pray in the synagogues and at the street corners, that they may be seen by men. Truly, I say to you, they have their reward. But when you pray, go into your room and shut the door and pray to your Father who is in secret; and your Father who sees in secret will reward you (Matt. 6:5-6).

There is within these words a refutation of the way God is described much of the time in the Old Testament. I did not say that there was a refutation of the God of the Old Testament, no indeed! In chapters 1 and 2 I attempted to show the inadequate concepts men then had of God. It was these concepts Jesus corrected by these words from Matthew 6 as well as in other statements.

I have found a large measure of real peace of mind in listing the assumptions taught by Jesus about God before I pray. I would advise that this is always a good pattern to follow. It is easier to appeal to someone if we rehearse his character in our minds. This being so in the sphere of human relations, how much more important it becomes for the God-man relationship.

119

1 When Jesus prayed he assumed first that God was all-knowing. He told his disciples, "Your Father knows what you need before you ask him." This came as somewhat of a revelation to the disciples. If they had surmised God's omniscience, they now could confirm it as truth. This knowledge can be a real lift to a distressed person. We don't have to inform God or, worse, convince him of the plight of the situation. One of the strengthening aspects in any human dilemma is that we take heart when our friends know of our needs. Their knowing is a mysterious source of strength. How much more satisfying it is for us that God knows. Jesus does not say God will agree with us about what we need to solve our predicament. What we think we need and what God knows we need could be different things. But it is a comforting thought that God knows what we need and is in control of the situation which brought about those needs.

2 Jesus prayed during moments of great stress but never did he indicate displeasure that God had allowed the stress to come. Rather, he would indicate that these things were for a greater purpose than was apparent at the moment. Since Jesus taught us that God knows all, let me suggest ways knowledge comes about. One way is to know by *observation*. We observe a distressing situation, and then we say that we know what the situation is like. This is only a half-truth. To observe a situation from a distance is not the

120

same as knowing the pain of those who are in it. Yet, we can honestly say when asked that we know, in the sense that we are apprised of the facts. There is knowledge which comes by *hearsay*, being told of a situation. Upon being asked at a later time we can again say that we know.

The third way men know is through *kindred experience*. We say that we know because "we have been where they are." I point us to the incarnation of God in Christ. God came to this earth uniquely in Jesus Christ. God was *in* Christ. Recognizing that we now can take heart as never before. God in Christ *knows* about us not as an observer of a news event or an onlooker at a spectacle of sorrow. He knows not as one who is told about our problems. It is the third category into which God fits. God created us and then became like us in his son. Jesus was "not unable to sympathize with our weaknesses" (Hebrews 4:15). God knows because he got inside our skin. He has "been where we are."

I don't know how this process works at all. It is impossible for me to prove to the father of a dead child that God can feel his pain as he experiences it, but somehow it is true. This is a mystery, yet quite believable. Somehow Jesus fully knows our sorrows, not as an observer of facts but as one who shares our experience. When we pray, we pray with this great assumption the ancients could not make.

121

The second assumption we can make when we pray is that God loves us. I suppose the grandest thrill which ever comes into the soul of any man is the thought that someone loves him. There is a power in this experience that defies human analysis. To know that just one person loves us is enough to alter the course of our lives, and most of us can point to several people who love us and whom we love. Like Jesus, we too can pray in this confidence—the full assurance that God loves us. This means that he wants what is best for us. Jesus never looked upon God as being capricious or vindictive, a god with a whip who was delighted with punishment. The grandeur of God's love is that man's sin can't diminish it.

The world is such a big feeling—yes, feeling. It is not a place in the strictest sense of the word. Man is not awed anymore by space and distance. Yet, with the hurdling of this barrier, finite man is still consumed by the bigness of it all. "What it all is" finds us without definition. There is a loneliness in that. The world is filled with lonely people, people who are lonely in the midst of a crowd. This is one indefinible quandary of human kind. It is really a loneliness that cries out for acceptance from beyond. It is a soul-hunger, a cry for help. This yearning of the inner man for communion with God finds an answer in the revelation, "God so loved the world." This theme was the stimulus for the writer of the Fourth Gospel.

122

Jesus made all men aware that God, this ultimate being, loves us. This presence, we know, is all around us and loves us. In keeping with this assumption of God's love, there is also God's care. He has unlimited concern for us. We cannot get beyond his love and care. When Jesus was going through the tragic hours of his last days, he was not unmindful of God's care. His statement on the cross about God's having forsaken him remains a mystery. Pious Jews would quote from the psalms in moments of anguish. The suffering of such excruciating pain must have made him feel as the psalmist felt when he wrote Psalm 22—Jesus was quoting the twenty-second psalm. The pain was driving him out of his mind as it would any man. Consequently, he, as a sufferer in great agony, could well have been articulating what many people feel in similar situations. When the body is collapsing in pain the best theology does not always surface. This aspect of Jesus' suffering means more to me as I see men suffer. So often people feel pain and express their anguish in terms of great doubt about God's role. Then they feel guilty, because they think that they have lost faith. This is not so, and it was not so with Jesus. Whatever urged him to utter this statement, it can in no way be considered a revelation of his theology of suffering.

I have known many people who have borne unbearable burdens, because they had the assurance that

God loved them. How well I remember a beautiful woman of sixty who had a terminal disease. Her words were poignant and real. Said she, "If you can assure me that God loves me and that he is not vindictive because of my sins, I can die in peace." I pointed out to her Jesus' death and the real physical suffering he endured. Physical suffering is a reality that we often sell short. When men hurt they don't think too rationally about anything, much less about God. When she was convinced of God's care and his love, she died in less than a day. Now here is a mystery. She was defying all odds by living a week longer than it seemed humanly possible. She hung on because she could not die believing in a God of retribution. She had not sinned any more than most people. That was not the point. Her problem was not moral or physical dissipation. She had a theological and philosophical problem she could not solve. She not only prayed that last night with the assurance that God loved and cared for her, but she died in this peace.

There is yet another assumption the Christian makes when he prays, the recognition of God's willingness to do good for his children, and Jesus makes this willingness very clear.

Ask, and it will be given you; seek, and you will find; knock, and it will be opened to you. For every one who asks receives, and he who seeks finds, and to him who knocks it will be opened. Or what man of you, if his son asks him for bread, will give him a stone? Or if he asks for a fish, will give him a serpent? If you then, who are evil, know how to give good gifts to your children, how much more will your Father who is in heaven give good things to those who ask him! (Matt. 7:7-11)

The essential thrust of this statement is not a play on the relationship of good gifts over bad gifts. The heart of this passage points to Jesus' conception of God. We should not read the passage with a crass literalism. If we do this we will be misled. On the surface it appears as if anything we ask for shall be given to us. Jesus does not qualify the statement at all. I think he omits qualification because he did not expect to be taken literally. That God would give us whatever we ask at a moment's notice is foolishness. We should value this passage for what it tells us about God. Jesus is simply saying that God wills good for his children. In other words, God is willing! This may seem to be of little significance, but it is of paramount importance. Contrast Jesus' assertion about God with a lot of modern-day prayer assumptions. Jesus says, "Let me tell you where God stands." The emphasis is not on the mechanics of asking; the emphasis is on the disposition of the one being asked. He is not saying, "Ask anything and God stands ready." He is saying, "God stands ready and willing to do good for his children."

At this point I want to debate seriously an ideology of miracle. The same folks I mentioned in chapter 3 are urging an unreal literalism regarding the prayer passages. They say that literally all we have to do is ask, seek, and knock. Here they are in trouble. The pitiful adherents to their views cry out, "I *have* been asking, seeking, and knocking. I am not healed, and my prayers for my loved ones are not granted." The leader is put in a tough spot. He or she turns the game of words around and says, "Well, sister, you don't have the faith." And off we go!

Previously we have mentioned that God, to some people, is a great power-substance in the sky. To them, faith is the electric current that starts the big turbine called God. Faith to them is a good vibration. When operative it hits the machine, the turbine starts, and away goes the sinus trouble, away go the crutches, etc. These if-you-have-faith people never define what they mean by faith. When they put the burden of definition on those poor people who put their hands on the TV or who travel miles to line up for a healer, it is patently unfair. They are talking **about faith in a** *quantitative* **manner:** "I've got a truckload of faith and you only have a jar full. My greater amount is the reason I get a miracle worked by the big Man (or the big machine). I have the best vibrations."

To proof-text this, the miracle-inducers turn to the famous passage about the mustard seed. This passage

126

has been as misunderstood as the one about asking and receiving.

He said to them, "Because of your little faith. For truly, I say to you, if you have faith as a grain of mustard seed, you will say to this mountain, 'Move from here to there,' and it will move; and nothing will be impossible to you" (Matt. 17:20).

In this passage a suffering little boy has to remain in his dilemma because of the inadequate faith of the disciples. On the surface it appears that the faith of one person becomes operative for another. Although one cannot fathom the entire scene, it is not as seems. It appears as if the child's future depended upon the fickleness of the disciples' faith. Since this is not the concept of God Jesus paints elsewhere, we should not read this meaning into the passage. It would be grossly unfair for a child's future to hinge upon a concept of faith which is measured in such crudeness as a truckload against a half-truckload. If that were the case, when would the right amount become operative? "How big a mustard seed?" we would have to ask. They are not all the exact same size. Can we measure one man's "adequate" faith over against the other poor soul's "inadequate" faith? Faith as an operative idea in this passage is not an easy thing to grasp, as we are sometimes led to believe.

This passage cannot possibly make sense unless the

term faith in it is defined. We must admit that the fate of little suffering children does to some degree hinge on other people. This is seen in the loving care of doctors, nurses, dentists, psychiatrists, ministers, teachers, parents, and others. In this sense God is waiting for the proper professional care. But to indicate that the cure of a person depends on faith defined as an unqualified feeling is to me absurd. Innocent and helpless people are put at the whims of someone else. God, too, is at the mercy of the whims of human beings. A drama with three participants seems to be required. A sick person and a willing God is not considered a workable equation unless a third party conjures up enough "something" to tap the power-source (called God).

I can't believe in this kind of a God, and in other passages Jesus eases our minds. He says God is not like this. I believe that the passage about the little boy which precedes the mustard statement has no reference to the tapping of God's power. It is not right to build a scheme of miracle-working on the scant outline here, although it is used in this misleading way.

There are many ways to define faith. When Jesus mentioned faith in this passage, he was not referring to faith as an activity of mood or emotions. Faith here seems to mean a frame of mind or proper thinking. Jesus is saying, "If you had had the proper understanding of the situation you could have removed this

128

mountain." Faith is a set of the mind. Thinking correctly about God is a true exercise of faith. Too often an exercise of faith is limited to some display of devotion. Not always so! I don't think Jesus was saying to the disciples, "If you men had worked your feelings up to an acceptable level you would have been able to release the power source." The passage is usually interpreted this way.

The child's real problem was emotional not physical. This particular scene would have been drastically changed if he had had one arm and needed another. But, his need was in another area. Obviously, the disciples approached the lad not knowing his real problem. The demon that was in him could well have been his own self-doubt and fear. I have counseled people with similar distresses. Along with Christian doctors and the use of medicine I have seen them improve and some "healed." However, never have I suggested that they had a demon that had crawled into their bodies. The disciples failed in that they could not identify the problem. The New English Bible calls it "epilepsy" in the Mark account (9:14-29). The disciples made the mistake that so many make. They tried to lump all problems under one heading. In this case demons was the category. The rise of belief in demons as causes for disturbance was not a Jewish idea but one the Jews had borrowed only a few hundred years before Christ. This explains the absence of the idea in the Old Testament, and, as pointed out earlier, could explain the disappearance of this belief in the early church.

The failure of the disciples was in their handling of the boy. The boy could see in their eyes that they didn't really believe they could help him. I can identify with their feeling; so can men in all generations. If I counsel a person or a doctor treats a person with the I-really-can't-help-you routine, the person can see it. On the other hand, if a person believes in the one who is trying to help him, a power is released. I have had to tell people that they would have to believe in their own ability to help themselves. Upon careful examination of this passage we see that God is not overtly brought into the situation. Jesus uses the idea of faith, but he does not mention God in this particular context. Here Jesus is talking about faith as something other than an activity directed toward God. He introduces the idea of faith as a proper way of thinking about God, as well as the child's problem. He is not talking about faith as an induced state of mental gymnastics or a traumatized, glassy-eyed condition. I don't see Jesus berating the disciples because they failed to dance around the child screaming for God to heal. I don't believe he was critical because the proper "vibes" were missing.

Now let us notice how Jesus handled the problem and how he plainly infers that the disciples could

130

have done the same thing. It says that Jesus spoke sternly to the child. It does not say that Jesus spoke harshly to the demon which was crawling around inside the boy. And yet, it is really one and the same. In Mark's account Jesus does address a "demon," obviously for the lad's benefit. Jesus probably took hold of the child, looked him straight in the eye and told him that he was well. He probably assured him that he was not going to have this problem of falling into the fire again. He made the child believe that there was no harm in the fire for the rest of his life, and thus he was healed. Nowhere in the passage is God brought into the picture as a power source. Yet it was God working through the father of the lad and God working through the insight of our Lord. Healing didn't call for a bolt of heavenly power. It called for some very earthy things, and for a positive approach on the part of those who cared for the boy. I see Jesus exorcising this demon by saying that it didn't actually exist. His statement to the demon was really his way of addressing the boy. By so doing he was telling the lad that there was no power in the fire that was reaching him.

My intent here is to say that the so-called faith that was lacking in this scene was not some intangible, psyched-up, quantitative mass of feeling. The God so described by Jesus is not limited to this stuff. The poor father of the story did the best he could. If God were limited to a conjured-up trust, this loving father had

131

enough of this for God to cure the little boy. Therefore beneath the surface God was not dependent upon faith as a strong desire on the part of the father or the disciples. He was dependent on a proper frame of mind on the part of those involved. This frame of mind was to be transferred to the boy. It is wrong to build a pattern of God's activity on this passage alone. He might need a different aspect of faith on another occasion.

The expect-a-miracle position makes great use of the assertion that God is limited unless miraculous changes take place. I contend that this is highly restrictive. It is popular theology and quite damaging. According to this mind-set, if measured miracles do not occur, God has been thwarted. The truth is that God's care and power can be seen in *all* situations. He cares for the sparrows, but they still fall out of the sky. He cares for the grass, but it continues to be burned as fuel. He cares for the lilies of the field, but the frost consumes them just the same. When standards are made whereby God's presence and power are measured, it is a terribly limiting procedure. God's activity cannot be measured by any one pattern.

I should also say that God is not mentioned as the object of faith in this passage. Jesus did not say, "If you have faith *in God* as small as a mustard seed." He said, "If you have faith. . . ." A definition of faith can be broadened to mean more than an attitude of prayer or a mood directed toward God. One can act in faith with proper thoughts and never go through the motions of petitioning the Father in heaven. This is important, because it broadens an area that the expect-a-miracle folks restrict. They always draw the conclusion that miracles are impeded because we don't believe strongly enough. When I hear some folks talk about believing strongly enough, they come across as saying that *feeling* is valid belief. They do not recognize the other connotations of faith, namely proper thinking.

Now in the mustard-seed passage, Jesus clearly refutes the miracle theology. The passage is usually interpreted literally to mean if we had faith as *big* as a grain of mustard seed we could move something (a mountain) even bigger. Here again we hear faith as something one can measure, as one weighs a mustard seed or walks off the dimensions of the mountain. It is at this point that we miss the symbolic meaning and start pursuing faith as measured feelings. Jesus is not saying that God is just sitting there in the sky like a huge dynamo humming away with more power than he can hold. He is not saying that God is just yearning for us to plug in our cord of faith so that he can roll a mountain into the sea. Or, if we can't get enough faith to do away with the entire mountain maybe we can plug into it enough to slough off part of the mountain. Even though this is ridiculous it is exactly the way the passage is preached much of the time. All I have done

133

is to carry the absurdity to its logical conclusion. Jesus did not intend for us to treat faith as a quantitative thing. Faith is a quality of trust.

Faith is presented as a frame of mind in the New Testament. It is a frame of mind predicated upon certain reliable facts. For example, the early church preached that Jesus died for our sins, that he was buried, and that he was raised the third day (I Corinthians 15:3, 4). This was the substance upon which men built faith. It was not a feeling or a state of mind induced by some ecstatic experience. It was a rational assent to historical fact. Feelings come as a result of belief.

When Jesus said, "If you have faith...," he was talking about confidence or trust in a set of facts. Now we have linked this passage to the basic assumptions Jesus used in prayer. Let us in this light treat the mustard-seed passage. By viewing faith as proper thinking which *can be* measured rather than as feelings which *can't be*, we can make sense out of it. Suppose you are struck blind. This is a real mountain for you. Or suppose you are told that you have a malignancy. Here is a horribly huge mountain. How should you appropriate faith here? After you have prayed to live, or you have prayed for a miracle, you come to the conclusion that you are to die (or that if blind you will never see again). If you listen to some of the "healers" you will live the rest of your life with the added burden of a guilt-complex. But suppose you think of faith as trust and confidence in God. Now I did not say confidence in his healing you. I said confidence in God. There is a difference in believing in God as long as you think that he is going to do something for you and in believing in him because he is what he is. Try to make the basic assumptions Jesus made. God

> knows your need
> loves you dearly
> cares for you completely
> wills good for you, and
> works in your behalf.

This does not mean that God will heal you, and let's face it, we are all going to die sooner or later. Healings and miracles are at best transient. If you can have confidence that Jesus told us the truth about God then this will build your faith. In God's love, in his care, in his good will for you, you and I still may have mountains of stress and suffering. Man will never solve this mystery of suffering. The important thing to know is the truth of what we have before us about God. The expect-a-miracle ideology makes skeptics of men. For example, if a miracle doesn't come about, is there something wrong with the "expect" aspect? The only conclusion we are left with is yes there is! How do we measure this "expect" attitude? How do we know we have it when it comes about? It would be impossible to take our spiritual temperature and say, "Eureka, I have the right amount of expectancy."

The truth of the matter is that when miracles do come they cannot be traced to any one observable set of procedures. Most folks who believe the "expect" idea are only painfully aware of the diagnosis that, whatever it is, they don't have it. Why? Because they didn't get a miracle. I must illustrate what I think to be the real meaning of the mustard-seed passage. I witnessed a woman who had been gullible and taken in by the God-manipulators. She was dying and wanting badly to live. She had tried the healer's prescription—the have-faith routine. Since she was dying she was convinced that either she didn't have enough faith, or that God was discriminating against her. This last idea was really a bigger mountain than her illness. She said to me, "I don't even have faith as big as a mustard seed." I said very calmly, "Your faith needs analyzing and defining first." We proceeded to define the word as I have done earlier. Then I asked her if she considered that she had *any* trust in these assumptions at all—the assumptions about God Jesus gave us. She thought for a while and said, "Yes, surely this is an accurate picture of God." I then asked her if she had confidence in this sketch of the nature of God, just enough confidence to equal a small seed as compared to a mountain. To this she brightened up and said that of a certainty she had at *least* that amount of faith (trust, confidence) to work on. I assured her that this small seed, rather than not being big enough, was more than large enough to move the mountain. I told her that the least amount of right-thinking about God was a virtual dynamo and that *this* was the true definition of faith.

I urged her to have faith in God—not in God's power. I told her that the idea she had been taught was wrong. What she had been taught was essentially mistrust of God. It was predicated on the idea that God's willingness was not assured. I told her that God was willing, that she could be assured that he willed nothing but good for her. However, she must understand that in the marvelous mystery of our relationship with him, it might not be his will or purpose that she should be healed. We then began to talk about the metaphors of the sparrows, the grass of the field, and the lilies. God cared for all these, yet all went through death. We talked about the nature of God. Her mustard seed grew and the next day she said a marvelous thing, "The mountain is cast into the sea!"

Here is real Christian theology and discipleship. Mountains can be removed by mustard seeds. They are removed every day. I think of a blind Viet Nam veteran whose essential trust in God has eliminated the mountain of blindness yet he is still blind. He said, "If I am miraculously healed that will be won-

137

derful, but as far as blindness is concerned, it is not a mountain." There is no mountain that cannot be removed by this kind of faith or trust in God. On the other hand, there is hardly a molehill that our feelings can take away. It then is comforting to know that faith is not feelings.

Jesus taught us to enter into prayer with these assumptions about God. It is better to pray thirty seconds with a proper concept of God than to pray all night with pagan notions about his power or his willingness to use this power for us. We find real confidence by going over these ideas *before* we pray. Doubt, distrust, spiritual neurosis, and twisted ideas are removed as faith is built. We no longer hazard dependency on mood levels.

In the beginning of this discussion I said that I intended seriously and candidly to debate the "if-you-have-faith" approach to prayer. Certainly that is the case, and I bear no personal ill will toward those who foster this attitude. I must say that I think they are hurting people. My pastoral concern causes me to be quite frank in my disagreement with them. Many of us as pastors, doctors, and other concerned Christians have to pick up the pieces after the expect-a-miracle idea has cooled off. Many folks who expected it and didn't get it are now bearing a double burden. At first they wrestled with pain and suffering. Now they wrestle with doubt and despair. They have misgivings about God. A man can bear the unbearable as a *Love* Christian, if he can know where God stands. Jesus *this* came to tell us where God stands, and it is a far cry from where he is pictured much of the time!

Jesus said that we could call God Father. If this was not a unique contribution of our Lord, it was certainly stressed more by him than by his contemporaries. If God is Father to me as I am to my children, then this very concept clears up much that is made confusing. I don't give good gifts to my children as a result of taking their temperatures to see if I can measure their faith in me as their father. I act for them according to fact, rational love and fatherly care. I never say, "Now, if you will have enough faith in me I will give you medicine for your sick body." I do what I can for them, because I am their father.

God as our Father does what he can for us. Here is the mystery of "what God can." Let it be, let it be! We should not want to know the inner counsels of God's thought. We as mortals could not hear these things. We live in faith, faith as trust. God's people ought to be getting help from a faith-to-die-by rather than pinning false hopes on a faith-to-get-well-by. Of this fact I am convinced.

A terrible phenomenon is arising in our midst. We are only now emerging from the frustrating state of warfare between the social and evangelical factions. We need both, as we have learned. However, a new

139

cleavage is upon us at this time. It is the cleavage between the rational and the emotional. A real effort is being made to sow distrust in the rational in religion. Weird things are happening which could initiate a new Dark Ages of Christian thought.

A perfect example of this is the emergence of "prayer language." The fact that Paul said he would pray with the mind *as well as* the spirit doesn't seem to deter this movement at all. Those who use this prayer language make noises like "goo, goo, goo" and "da, da, da." They admit that in this trance-like condition they are unaware of what they are saying. A United States senator told me within this past year that several of his friends had insisted that he get this "gift" and until he did, he would not know real prayer. Let's analyze this for a minute. Prayer language is in reality a refutation of scripture. If we are unaware of what we are saying, we can't be praying with the mind, as Paul instructed. In this case, the praying one is a mere puppet. He is a thing upon which God weaves a spell. Since he is unaware of what he is praying, then God (as the only one who is aware) is talking to himself. This is absurd! Jesus nowhere practiced such things. If God is Father then he certainly wants us to be intelligent and intelligible in our communication with him. It would be patently absurd for me to want to keep one of my children in a stage of infantile communication that is amusing to

Author's idea of
what Jesus
taught us about
God

me as a parent but is detrimental to my child. Prayer language is another one of the neo-charismatic fruits which is virtually destroying any attempt toward sanity in man's spiritual dimension. We would do well to ignore it. Our Lord taught us some marvelous things about God. He taught us theism in place of atheism whose God is not there. He taught us theism in place of agnosticism whose God does not care. Prayer in Jesus' mind was the intelligent grasp of man's link with the Father. It is not enhanced by a state of trance. The heathen practice all about him the first century stressed such ideas.

Prayer is then, essentially the articulation of knowledgeable trust. It can be accomplished through mere thought processes. To think correctly about God, as Jesus taught us, is to foster within us this thing called faith. Actually, to think right is to pray, for correct thinking leads to trust. The end result of all true Christian praying is unbounded trust in God!

Some would ask why men should pray to an all-knowing God. This is a better question than how to pray to an all-powerful God, because the "how to" usually borders on gimmickry. If my life is in the hands of the kind of God Jesus characterized, then why pray to him? I can think of many reasons: for reflection, communion, meditation, and baring of the soul. However, there is one I would mention above all, praying for instruction. By taking our requests to

141

God after we rehearse the assumptions Jesus gave us, our faith is strengthened. Also, it draws us closer to God our Father. When I take my burdens to God while at the same time I summarize his nature and disposition to me as Jesus told us, I come away from prayer a different person. I may not come away with my requests answered, but I have grown in a greater degree of love and confidence in the one Jesus called Father. I have thus been to the school of true praying.

It is because God is omniscient that prayer is so important. When we pray to this kind of being we come away with a better insight into ourselves. In other words, we not only see the situation better, but we see into ourselves in some measure as God sees us. For example, some people have been able to accept themselves for the first time, because they found out that God loves them.

I have been richly blessed in knowing some of God's choicest servants who have endured suffering. Through the years I have been moved emotionally as I looked out over the congregations and knew the depth of love many of these suffering ones had for God. They present a much better picture of intense Christian discipleship than throngs of people lined up in feverish anticipation at the feet of the healers.

Surely it was not the expect-a-miracle idea which the writer had in mind in that great hymn of affirmation, This Is My Father's World. We should follow the

142

development of thought carefully. It rings with true Christian perspective. The miracle greater than all others is the very fact that this world belongs to our Father.

> This is my Father's world,
> And to my listening ears
> All nature sings, and round me rings
> The music of the spheres.
> This is my Father's world:
> I rest me in the thought
> Of rocks and trees, of skies and seas;
> His hand the wonders wrought.
>
> This is my Father's world,
> The birds their carols raise,
> The morning light, the lily white,
> Declare their maker's praise.
> This is my Father's world:
> He shines in all that's fair;
> In the rustling grass I hear him pass,
> He speaks to me everywhere.
>
> This is my Father's world,
> O let me ne'er forget
> That though the wrong seems oft so strong,
> God is the ruler yet.
> This is my Father's world:
> Why should my heart be sad?
> The Lord is King: let the heavens ring!
> God reigns: let the earth be glad! Amen.

This was the way Jesus taught men to perceive God's concern for his children. May it ever be.